RUNNING FROM SHADOWS

www.runningfromshadows.com
www.runningfromshadowsdotcom.wordpress.com

RUNNING FROM SHADOWS

MY MARATHON DES SABLES

MARK ROE

FOREWORD BY RORY COLEMAN

71

Matador
9 Priory Business Park
Kibworth Beauchamp
Leicestershire LE8 0RX, UK
Tel: (+44) 116 279 2299
Fax: (+44) 116 279 2277
Email: books@troubador.co.uk
Web: www.troubador.co.uk/matador

ISBN 978-1783064-007

British Library Cataloguing in Publication Data.
A catalogue record for this book is available from the British Library.

Typeset in Aldine by Troubador Publishing Ltd
Printed and bound in the UK by TJ International, Padstow, Cornwall

Matador is an imprint of Troubador Publishing Ltd

To my wife, Emma: without your constant love and support over the years all the training and all these achievements would have been immensely harder.

And to my nephew and niece, Noah and Zoe: always chase your dreams.

Contents

Foreword

There's something quite magical about the Marathon des Sables that you simply can't put into words. It's simply more than awesome. It must be, as I return to it year-on-year to conquer the western Sahara desert, one of the fiercest environments known to man.

The 'race' is more of a 'journey' for most of the 1000+ runners that reach the start line to set off running, walking or crawling the 150 miles of sand and mountains, carrying everything they need in a rucksack in temperatures of 50 degrees centigrade or more.

Each year I meet and train hundreds of people from the UK to reach that goal of earning one of the most prestigious medals in the ultra-marathon running world. Funnily enough, when they return home, no-one will ask them how long it took them to do the race or where they came, just "Did you finish?"

It's a race where everyone who finishes is a winner and there's a complete spectrum of athletic abilities and all manner of shapes and sizes and nationalities of people taking part. The entry criteria is more about the ability to pay for the race and the specialist lightweight kit one needs and having a healthy ECG test rather than the ability to run a sub-3 hour marathon.

Is it tough?

It's relentless. It tests everyone who enters from the first to the last and provides every competitor with a real Everest of a challenge. What the race does provide inadvertently, however, is a physical and mental 'journey' of personal rediscovery.

While training for but more so during and after the race competitors get the chance to re-evaluate their lives. It's an extremely cathartic process which I thoroughly enjoyed when I first ran the race in 1999 and have enjoyed each time I've returned to the desert. The race is a real 'life laundry' as it's a break from busy jobs, schedules, home-lives, mobile phones and the internet.

I thought I met Mark for the first time in the lead-up to the MdS in early 2012 but we actually met before that during a six-hour track race in Sheffield, just two weeks after my first MdS in April 1999. Quite uncanny that. Mark's MdS journey was one which I found fascinating to watch and it's one that stood out for me that year as he went from really questioning himself, his reason for living and his reason for being, to emerge with a new life philosophy, fresh horizons and new life standards to live by.

It's marvellous that he can share his journey with us and his account of the Marathon des Sables, the 'toughest footrace on Earth'. If you've been there you'll understand just what it's like and if you haven't then maybe you should.

Rory Coleman

Rory Coleman: Performance Coach
815 Marathons, 218 ULTRA-marathons, 9 Guinness World Records & 10 Marathon des Sables
Photo © Rory Coleman

1

Running from Shadows

June 2009

"But you can't stand the heat!"

This was true.

"You suffered in the heat in that race in Doncaster, for God's sake!"

This was also true, a reference to my second 24 Hour running race in Doncaster in 2002. Unseasonably hot daytime temperatures and a midday start saw me sunburnt, dehydrated and exhausted by 6pm. I slept a lot of those 24 hours and instead limped home with 63 miles in my legs (a disappointment after the 81 miles achieved in the 2000 event).

My wife was making perfectly valid points.

We were on holiday with my in-laws, including my sister-in-law's niece and nephew who had already exhausted me with their demands for swimming challenges in the pool. In June in Majorca the early afternoon sun had peaked to give a temperature in the mid-30C; the surrounding landscape was desert-like, with parched, cracked ground and barely-alive shrubs. As I was on holiday it was a now unfortunately rare opportunity to go out for a run and try yet another attempt to get my fitness back, so long ago lost.

I hadn't lasted long. Returning after half an hour I was a bit of a wreck: my body had almost entirely forgotten how much faster I used to run years before; but my mind hadn't and thought my body was far more capable of turning over my legs than it was actually physically capable of doing. I returned to the villa burnt, sweating profusely, my kit soaked, more dehydrated than I was just half an hour ago.

This wasn't a surprise: I hadn't exercised regularly for almost four years.

I'd been unhappy of late about my lost fitness and misdirected focus in my life. On this run I found myself injected urgently with an insane idea that would rebalance my focus once again. Back at the villa I'd blurted out to my wife:

"I'm thinking about running the Marathon des Sables: what do you think?"

The initial reaction wasn't entirely positive.

★ ★ ★

It hadn't always been like this. In my early 20s in the early 1990s I'd joined my local amateur rugby union club off the back of the euphoria sweeping the UK from a successful second Rugby Union World Cup. I'd enjoyed battering and getting battered on a Saturday afternoon for a few years. The positions I'd played developed in proportion to my growing physique: I started out successfully as a number 14 winger, in one of my early matches scoring a hat-trick of tries against a team that hadn't been beaten in five years. The following season after a summer of good food saw me progress into the position of centre; a couple of seasons later, after confusing a perception of fitness with meaning I could eat whatever I liked, I was battered even more regularly in various roles in the scrum: flanker, prop, hooker. From lightweight winger to heavyweight forward in a few years.

Belatedly, university beckoned. In my first season there the university club gave the nod that I was doing well in helping them make decisions about who to send off for trials to try and join the England University rugby union team. That was until an idiot buried his head with force into my lower back in a maul. In agony my rugby playing days were over; almost a year of rehabilitation followed before I could get moving properly again.

That period led to inevitable weight gain. How to shift it?

An old school friend of mine had the view that if I hadn't taken up some form of exercise by the time I was 25 I was destined to a life of porkiness that would make it ever more difficult to keep fit. I'd thought at the time rugby would be the answer, but with hindsight that would never have been for long. As he was training for that year's London Marathon I decided to train for the same thing. I would never be more than a mid- to back-of-the-pack runner but the point for me was to enjoy it along the way. Little did I know that this would mark the beginning of trying for the ever-longer distance.

26.2 miles: it's a very long way to go by foot.

The training went well. The weight dropped off, but only a little. It would be many, many years yet before I learnt that training didn't mean I could eat what I liked, that fuel going in has a lot to do with performance coming out.

But my fitness improved. I was introduced to repetitions and hill training. I was jubilant at having run for one hour without stopping, for the first time, on a cold, dark, autumn evening in 1995: I remember this milestone very well. I built my running to complete my first London Marathon, painfully, in 1997.

I joined the legions of other first-time marathon finishers and swore never to do another again.

But after a short while I wondered if I could do it faster. Forgetting the pain I decided to have another go and try to break four hours for the London Marathon. Exhausted, I managed it in my second London Marathon in 1998, according to my stopwatch: 3 hours, 54 minutes. My official time was just outside four hours on the clock but this was before the days of electronic chip recording that would take into account the 15 minutes it would take to reach the start line.

So I knew I could run a marathon. But what else?

As a regular subscriber to the magazine *Runner's World* I marvelled at some of the ridiculous extremes some runners would go to. I read an article about one particularly bonkers race, some 150 miles unsupported across the Sahara desert. Something called the Marathon des Sables. Not a chance. It was never on my radar. I enjoyed reading the article but it was purely an inspiration for me to achieve my own more modest goals.

★★★

The year 1998/1999, a year before I would return to full-time work, became a golden period from a personal athletic point of view.

Back home having graduated from university in the glorious summer of 1998 I dropped in to the local leisure centre to try the town's Concept II Indoor Rowing Challenge. With barely a week or two of training for it I won both my age group category and the event as a whole over 2000 metres at the highest and hardest Level 10, beating the town's entire Fire Brigade entrants in the process. I entered the British Indoor Rowing Championships held a couple of months later and was pleased with my effort (I didn't though beat Greg Searle, the Olympic medallist, who was in the same wave of competitors as me…).

Having graduated from university I was now at law college, on the road to qualifying as a solicitor, where I met my wife. She was introduced on one of our first dates to a personality that didn't understand stopping or giving up: the first race I finished with her supporting me was my inaugural George Littlewood Six Hour Challenge running round and round the 400-metre track in the Don Valley Stadium in Sheffield in April 1999. It was an enjoyable race, meeting, passing and being passed by a number of people who would become friends over subsequent editions of the race. But in this first attempt acute Achilles tendon pain saw me taking

Ibuprofen like Smarties rather than stop. My wife-to-be, although neither of us knew that at the time, looked concerned, wondering no doubt what she'd let herself in for: on the way home I kept asking to pull over onto the hard shoulder of the M1 so I could vomit. Several times.

But that was off the back of having run my fastest ever half marathon at the Ackworth Half Marathon in 1 hour, 37 minutes, 46 seconds. In these months I felt invincible.

An Ironman-distance triathlon sounded like a good idea to extend my boundaries. In the late-1990s the distinctive official American Ironman brand hadn't yet hit UK shores; that wouldn't come until 2005. Instead, the Black Country Triathletes club had for years held their own brand of a 2.4 mile swim, a 112 mile cycle polished off with a 26.2 mile marathon run in the Midlands: the Longest Day Triathlon. Tick: completed on a hot August day in a pleasing 13 hours, 38 minutes.

A few months later I started my training contract in a City law firm and resolved to persist with my physical pursuits: I enjoyed the addiction of training and competing with others in the middle of the field. The marathons and half-marathons I completed continued to increase in number. I completed my second Longest Day Triathlon in 2000, somehow fitting in the training after long working hours and a long commute. Returning home at 9 pm to go for a 10 to 15 mile run wasn't much fun but I was determined to get my second Longest Day Triathlon nailed. I did it, but slower than the first.

My enjoyment of completing these challenges was starting to reduce in proportion to the amount of time I was increasingly spending commuting or at work. I kept running for as long as I could. I was never a front-runner, always heavier than I should have been, but I enjoyed the extremes, running with like-minded amateurs who also had day-jobs that no-one ever talked about: there was no need to in the camaraderie of racing against oneself.

★ ★ ★

A poor diet, poor sleeping patterns, long working hours and long commutes ensued. None of this was conducive to continuing what I enjoyed. A few years passed; my earlier successes at a younger age came because of the robustness given by relative youth; as time passed, so did youth and its ability to repair my body quickly.

Inevitably the injuries started to arrive: Achilles tendon and plantar fasciitis issues forced an early retirement from the 2002 edition of the George Littlewood Six Hour Challenge, which was sadly my last. Poor core stability would take months of physiotherapy to resolve. Too much heel-strike road running created years of pain and discomfort in my Achilles tendons. I desperately tried to find solutions, seeing a variety of podiatrists, sports masseurs and physiotherapists with varying degrees of success that didn't last. The weekly miles had dropped off almost completely by late 2004.

I needed a new resolve, a new goal, to get me back on track.

It had come with the announcement that the official Ironman brand was coming to the UK. This inaugural official Ironman would be held around Sherbourne in Dorset on Sunday 21 August 2005.

Could I swim, bike and run 140.6 miles in one day for a third time? I was still commuting and still working long hours. The injuries refused to clear up. I was tired all the time. My Achilles tendons were constantly sore and tight: I felt much like an 80 year old must feel getting out of bed first thing on a morning.

But I *would* finish my third Ironman-distance triathlon. Overweight and nowhere near as fit as I once was I did finish the 2005 event in a poor 16 hours, 16 minutes, some 44 minutes before the cut off time. It was a very uncomfortable 16 hours: I had cut the ball of my foot on the lake's rocks on emerging from the lake swim, spending the next 138 miles hiding my bloody foot from the marshalls; my foot was a painful, squidgy mess at the finish.

Although I was ecstatic at crossing the finish line, impressed by the winner of the event, New Zealander Bryan Rhodes, still there some 8 hours after he finished giving out finisher's medals as they crossed the line, I silently resolved to myself... *that's it. That's the end; I can't do this stuff anymore*.

I tried to restart but my training world was an apocalyptic one of howling winds and rolling tumbleweed. I told myself I would try to lose weight, I would do a little to try and give a nod to some semblance of fitness, but I was in the world of eat, work, eat, sleep.

I was done with trying to serve two masters.

★ ★ ★

We'd been home a week from our Majorcan holiday. The UK was experiencing a rare true summer. It was hot and, as I was painting the fence, it got hotter in the blazing sunshine. I hadn't really thought much more about the Marathon des Sables since mentioning it to my wife on my return from that scorching run. Sat painting in the heat I remembered that hot short run and the possibility of the Marathon des Sables appeared in my thoughts again.

I'd completed my third and last Ironman-distance triathlon at Sherbourne almost four years ago. *Four years*. Where had it gone?

And what had I done in the meantime?

Nothing. Zilch. The odd short walk. The odd short run. I hadn't entered nor completed any event of any description in that time.

How did I feel?

I was too heavy for a start. Recently I'd been hitting the scales at 16 stone, the heaviest I'd been in my lifetime.

The recession we were in that had started a couple of years ago and which would be over in a few months, so everyone assumed, meant my working hours were mostly less than they used to be; but for a multitude of reasons I wasn't enjoying what I was doing.

My muscles felt tired, tight and sore. My Achilles tendons still ached; on occasion I could still barely move when first getting up on a morning.

I was grouchy and my wife noticed it. She'd been saying for some time that I needed to get back into the habit of what I used to enjoy. I felt a hole but didn't know what it was that would fill it, even though the answer, given by my athletic history, was there all the while staring back at me.

I could feel the longing to do something, a desperate urge to get back what I used to enjoy: the ability to conquer extremes with others like-minded.

But what would spur me on now? I'd already completed a couple of 24 hour races, several 6 hour races, numerous marathons and half-marathons and three Ironman-distance triathlons. Doing those again didn't really interest me.

I was in a deep rut. I realised I really should start to do something. If I didn't the shadows of middle-aged ailments would begin to cast and maybe they already were. I could see them around work colleagues of all ages and generally amongst the UK populace: negativity; a lack of fulfillment from working life; sleep-deprivation; adult-onset Type 2 diabetes; obesity; later, inevitably, far worse. I wanted to run from these shadows for as long as I physically could.

Painting the fence in a Zen-like concentration had given me the time to think and I started to figure that maybe training for the Marathon des Sables and trying to complete it was the spur that I needed to turn things around.

I put down my paint brush. A sudden urgency took me… *this was the answer!*

I prepared myself a late lunch and settled in front of the laptop for the rest of the afternoon and on late into the night. I read all I could about the Marathon des Sables, all that I needed to allow me to reach a decision.

★ ★ ★

The man synonymous with the Marathon des Sables, the Marathon of the Sands in its English translation and known in its abbreviated form as the MdS, is its creator, Patrick Bauer.

In 1984 Patrick, a concert promoter and said to be a former French Foreign Legionnaire, decided to go for a walk: 200 miles across the Sahara desert with just whatever he could carry on his back. Purified after his journey, he wanted to recreate the experience for others: the Marathon des Sables was born.

It took two years to organise and raise the financing to allow the inaugural Marathon des Sables to take place in 1986. A close relationship has built up over the years between Patrick and the King of Morocco, such that the event has been staged annually since its beginning.

Just 23 competitors toed the line for that first event in 1986 at a time when little could be learnt about the event, when shoes and kit choices were primitive compared with today's ever-developing standards. By 2012 and after 27 editions of the event some 13,000 competitors had completed this gruelling race.

Now, the event is an annual international affair entered by all manner of amateurs, professionals, armed forces personnel (the French Foreign Legion particularly), regular runners and those who have never run a marathon. The 2012 race saw a record number of countries of the world represented at the event; those countries with new appointed representative offices of the MdS continue to expand as the event grows with Australia and Scandinavia joining that list in 2012.

The statistics of the race make impressive and interesting reading: 30% of entrants have completed it before; the average maximum speed is 14 kilometres per hour with the average minimum speed being 3 kilometres per hour. In the 2012 event the youngest competitor was 16 with the oldest at 80 years of age. The

80 year old competitor called his 2012 event his last… his seventh completion.

Few run the entire event with 90% alternating running and walking, signifying the impossibility for the majority of the field of running the entire course; 10% walk the whole distance.

The longest stage, Stage 4, is around 50 miles with a 36 hour time limit but weather disaster in the 2009 event saw this stage at a record 57 miles to help make up for some cancelled stages. Most seek to complete this stage by carrying on through the night to reach the finish rather than suffer yet another day of being boiled alive in the sun.

With the final Stage 6 commonly being a "fun run" of around 10 miles across the steepest sand dunes Morocco has to offer, and Stage 5 being the traditional marathon stage, Stages 1 to 3 commonly range between 18 and 25 miles each.

It's a long way. The event has been tagged over many years as "the toughest footrace on Earth" but with other events having appeared since 1986 no-one can now agree with any certainty what that is.

What is beyond doubt is that even some of the most accomplished of the world's ultra-runners can fail to complete this demanding race: temperatures in almost every edition of this race exceed 50C; the total race distance is traditionally around 250 kilometres or 156 miles, a high proportion of it across sand depending on the year's route, which changes annually. It's a race for which entry includes a compulsory fee for corpse repatriation: competitors over the years have indeed become lost, become seriously injured or died.

Many may have heard of the story of the Italian policeman Mauro Prosperi. In the 1994 race Mauro became disorientated and lost in a severe sand storm where the ground and the air merged into a sandy single mass. Without any tracks, and forgetting the golden desert rule to stay put until the storm passed, he wandered lost for nine days. He was finally discovered in a hospital in the neighbouring country of Algeria having lost some 18 kg in weight having lived on dead bats and drinking his own urine.

At one point it had become all too much: knowing he was destined for a grim death and feeling near the end after three days he found some shelter in a small abandoned mosque. Figuring his family would eventually find him here he slit his wrists and went to sleep to die.

Fortunately his dehyrated state ensured his blood quickly coagulated. Waking in the morning he resolved to stay alive. Five days later he was picked up by nomads in Algeria.

After a time to recover Mauro applied to run the MdS again but was refused and only accepted to run on his second application. He has since completed the MdS a number of times.

Others have become lost for a shorter period with less dramatic consequences, albeit frightening all the same. In an interview in 2012 for the irunfar website Patrick Bauer recounted to the eventual 2013 MdS women's winner Meghan Hicks how an English competitor had got lost one afternoon during a long, hot stage. Although the search continued overnight there was little more that could be done. The following morning the event helicopter took off to find the lost competitor. Spotting her saviour, the competitor launched her distress flare. She was then brought back to the start... just in time to begin that day's stage.

Unfortunately the race has claimed two lives in its history.

In 2007 49 year old Frenchman Bernard Julé, a previous MdS finisher, had finished the 50 mile long stage in 45th place, coming in to the bivouac in the early evening of the day he'd started, an unusual feat. After a rest he was awake in the dark very early hours of the following morning to greet some of his other tent mates back from their own desert hell. He returned to sleep in anticipation of a full day's rest prior to Stage 5; his tent mates woke up to begin the day just a few hours later and were horrified to find that

Bernard was dead: Bernard had died in his sleep of a heart attack despite being a very fit man with no history of illness.

The only other death has been of a 28 year old Frenchman who collapsed and died on a sand dune, again of a heart attack, in the 3rd edition of the MdS in 1988 during a stage where the temperature is said to have hit 56C.

With, annually, numerous injuries from the minor to the serious the MdS is a race that must be treated with the utmost respect.

⋆⋆⋆

I soon found that, unbelievably, I could only pay a deposit in July 2009 to get one of the few places that were left on the waiting list for the 2012 edition of the race. For any other country in the world it was possible to get MdS entry at relatively short notice but, such was the UK demand, places sold out years in advance. The few hundred confirmed places for 2012 had already gone a few months ago in half an hour from when the application website opened. It did though seem that the chances of actually going were very high if you could get into the top 100 on the waiting list.

Nervous energy mixed with excitement I completed my online application form and paid my £500 deposit.

A day or two later I received the email that made me take a deep breath: I was now on the waiting list in the top 90 for the 2012 edition of the Marathon des Sables.

Although the event was just under three years away it was time to think about training. Already I had the sense and feelings I needed to feel: that a challenge was coming, something so different from what I had done before.

I had no idea at the time what a life-changing experience this would turn out to be.

2

Getting There: A Plan, Rehab, Training and Heat

A Plan

July 2009 until April 2012: I had under three years to prepare as best I could to complete the 27th Marathon des Sables. I would need to get off the waiting list and onto the confirmed entrant list and that may not happen until a few months before the race. I knew though I couldn't leave my training to begin until I was, hopefully, confirmed in late 2011: that would be the road to an Abandonment classification against my name. I had plenty of time but I couldn't afford to let it slip by.

I reviewed my state of fitness: I was too heavy and would need to lose some weight. Having been horrified at recently tipping the scales at 16 stone I had lost a few pounds but I would need to lose plenty more. My sore, stiff, aching Achilles tendons would need to be sorted out as best they could: there was no way I'd get through the training I needed to do over the next couple of years and remain injury-free unless I got that resolved.

I was tired. This was probably a combination of being overweight and continuing to eat and drink rubbish, with a dash of sleeping poorly. I would need to change my eating habits and remind myself that good rest was as important as the physical training.

It became clear from internet research on training for the MdS that, firstly, there was very little agreement on the best training approach other than on very broad principles (for example, that a few fast half marathons would be nowhere near enough).

Secondly, there were certain elements to the MdS that would mean I had to tailor my training in a particular way. For starters I would be self-sufficient for the entire race. I would need to carry everything I needed on my back plus the water supplied by the organisers throughout each day: food, clothing, sleeping and cooking equipment. I would need to spend hours researching what that would consist of. There was of course the compulsory kit I would need to carry but I would also need to test all sorts of items along the way: rucksacks, shoes, freeze-dried meals, tops, everything. This could be expensive.

To carry all this stuff for a week upper body strength training would be necessary.

It seemed logical too that once I built up a base of fitness I would at some point, probably with a few months to go before the start of the race, in order to avoid injury and burn-out, have to introduce long-distance back-to-back run and walking efforts… with a fully laden rucksack. It seemed pointless doing this on roads and tarmac: I wouldn't see any across the Sahara desert.

My main concern was preventing injury. I knew from experience my body started to break down after three or four runs in a week. They would have to be quality runs and walks and I resolved to try and keep my training to not more than that number per week.

I had time on my side and before long had put together a broad plan:

- lose weight;
- stretch muscles regularly;
- gradually reintroduce running and walking with not more than a 10% weekly increase in mileage;
- build total distance and time over an escalating three week cycle

with the fourth week for doing what little I felt like doing and use that week to recover;
- try and sleep better;
- eat better;
- complete a marathon in the autumn of 2011;
- thereafter start introducing back-to-back runs and walks with a rucksack, building my peak week mileage to somewhere between 50 and 70 miles.

I wasn't particularly concerned about whatever would be the distance for the Stage 4 long stage, which would be somewhere around 50 to 55 miles. I knew from my previous 24 hour race efforts, albeit many years ago now, I should easily be able to cover 50-odd miles within what sounded like a generous cut-off time of some 36 hours. I didn't know though what it would be like in temperatures exceeding 50C over rough sandy terrain. I figured though that I would rediscover my mental resolve through my physical training; adding it to sheer bloody-mindedness would help and I felt that a confidence-boosting 30 to 40 mile outing a few months before the MdS would be all I needed.

But first I needed to sort myself out. After four years of inactivity I needed to be able to get up out of bed first thing on a morning and move fluidly without crippled, shortened Achilles tendons.

I was really starting my journey afresh, from zero, the muscle memory and mental resolve built on my previous years of efforts by now just mental vapours hanging around a 38 year old heavy frame.

★ ★ ★

Rehabilitation

If I was going to have to run a very long way I wasn't going to be able to do it with my old habit of heel-strike running. I did start doing so for a few weeks but those old heel-strike habits simply allowed the old grumbles let me know they were still there: my Achilles ached, my lower back ached, my running didn't feel fluid.

I needed to change how I ran to clear myself of the injuries and the tight, damaged muscles I had.

The book *Born to Run* had been causing a sensation in 2009. Christopher McDougall had suffered his own litany of injuries and sought solutions but failed to find them amongst his own list of physiotherapists and podiatrists. He had though heard of the Tarahumara Indians of Mexico who, it was said, ran for sometimes hundreds of miles either barefoot or with flimsy cut-offs from car tyres… without apparent injury.

So began Christopher's research which led to the publication of *Born to Run*. While I barely managed to eke out a few miles of running a week (there was no need to panic about my impending Marathon des Sables, just yet) I absorbed his book for every nuance that would help me to run freely.

After finishing an entertaining book I then decided that I too could become a Tarahumara Indian, bouncing up and down the Yorkshire Dales barefoot or in a pair of some weird-looking five finger toe shoes called Vibram Five Fingers, wearing traditional Tarahumaran Indian dress.

But first I needed to build up to this on a treadmill.

Without having to adopt Tarahumaran Indian dress it worked, for a short spell. It was true that running in a pair of socks on a treadmill, rather than with clunky running shoes, forced me to run up on my toes rather than landing on my heels. I could see it made sense that the natural way to run was barefoot on the front of the foot.

After a couple of months I accepted that my body's natural foot mechanics had given way to 39 years of tarmac and concrete. My calf muscles had become extremely tight and sore; the actual running (almost) barefoot felt fluid but for hours afterwards my calf muscles complained about the punishment they'd been put through.

Barefoot running up on my toes or forefoot was not going to work for me. I could though see something in changing my foot strike, to move away from putting three times my body's weight from running impact through my heels. But to what?

I scoured the internet to learn more and came across a compromise: a mid-foot running strike with a quicker cadence. I took a few weeks off towards the end of 2009 to allow the effects of my painful forefoot strike experiment to heal.

It was early 2010 and I still had just over two years to get fit enough for the MdS. The mid-foot striking went well as I stuck with it through the year (although I'd long given up on trying to do it barefoot on a treadmill).

Christmas was fast approaching: my weight wasn't moving much and was stuck stubbornly at just above 15 stone. Progress, but not enough. While my new mid-foot running strike felt immeasurably easier than heel-striking ever had my Achilles still weren't right. Towards the very end of 2010, having barely got above ten miles per week of running at any point that year and with many weeks still doing nothing at all, I finally resolved to seek help.

★ ★ ★

The question was: who should I ask? I approached this task with a groan: I'd had previous history with physiotherapists and other "medical practitioners" who couldn't provide any solutions.

After a few internet searches and recommendations I came across Dr. Martyn Speight. An accomplished fell runner himself Dr. Speight had begun his career as a musculoskeletal and sports physician having experienced frustrations as an NHS patient with the usual athletic injuries. I felt confident he'd be the man to sort me out.

Refreshingly I was given a diagnosis and suggested programme of rehabilitation in my first visit. A no-nonsense true Yorkshireman, the Doctor took notes, prodded and enquired and took an ultra-sound scan. After half an hour I had every confidence that my problems would be solved.

"You have what we call an Achilles tendinopathy. You may need orthotics. For now, do these exercises twice a day for three weeks. No running or walking for three weeks."

Sorted.

The good news was that I needn't run or walk through the cold and the snow of January 2011. What was not so good news was that there were now only 15 months before I was hoping to fly out to toe the start line of the Marathon des Sables.

★★★

By the spring of 2011 I could feel a significant improvement in my Achilles tendons: I could get out of bed and walk, for a start. I hadn't been able to do so regularly for a long, long time. I wasn't running more than a few times a week but by the summer I wasn't far off running 20 miles a week. I lost a few more pounds in weight. But my leg muscles weren't as comfortable as I felt they could be.

I hadn't had a decent sports massage for years. The thought of one made me wince. The joining of the words "sports" and "massage" into one term is important: this is no ordinary massage.

Again, the problem was finding a thorough sports masseur. I was pointed in the direction of Jim Mason, a highly qualified Member of the Sports Massage Association... who has worked on the England Rugby League training camp... who has worked on the Leeds Rhinos rugby league team.

I gulped in anticipation when I booked my first appointment.

I gulped a second time when I finally met Jim in anticipation of the pain to come: at 6 foot, looking strong and the size of a truck, this was going to hurt.

It did. The assessment was that my right calf in its deepest muscle was knotted and extremely tight, my left calf less so, and my illiotibial band, both of them, were tight too. It was a tough session full of expletives from me. After half an hour I got up off the table drenched in sweat and barely able to walk.

So I booked myself in for two sessions a week for a couple of months.

★★★

The only thing left that I could do to try and finally address the problems in my lower legs was to take an assessment for whether I needed orthotics in my running shoes. Dr. Speight referred me to Andrew Horwood, a specialist podiatrist. A quick assessment showed that, yes, I was overpronating a little, my feet rolling in slightly too far in the running but not the walking gait.

In less than an hour I left with a new pair of orthotics to keep my feet running in a straight line, far cheaper and more effective than any of the one or two pairs I'd tried in previous years. They gave almost immediate relief.

★★★

Thus by the end of the summer 2011 I was finally largely cured of long-term lower leg problems that had plagued my previous years of running: a combination of sticking to the exercises prescribed by Dr. Speight, a weekly sports massage battering or two and my new orthotics saw me pretty much free of lower leg tightness and discomfort. Which was a good job with just a few months now left to train.

It was time to turn on the training tap.

★★★

Training

Other than a few press-ups and lifting a few light weights my upper body training was minimal. I trusted that would be taken care of by, when I eventually did so in my plan, carrying a weighted rucksack for miles.

I discovered the Long Distance Walkers Association's (LDWA) "Challenge" events which meant these were open to runners as well as walkers. I knew that I needed to get the bulk of my walking and running off-road rather than pounding out the miles on tough tarmac so the LDWA events would prove to be invaluable for this purpose.

My first such event was a scenic but hilly 16 mile jaunt with a 4 kg rucksack in the Durham Dales Challenge in June 2011. A hot, humid day saw me finish very tired and dehydrated but it was enjoyable nonetheless. At this point I'd finally been able to hit the elusive 20 miles per week without any injury or tightness in my lower legs.

As the summer progressed the miles increased. I sought to follow a three week build up with a one week recovery of doing whatever I liked (sometimes nothing) but, as is the case with best laid plans, I didn't always achieve it. I also kept the impact damage low by introducing walking breaks during my runs: I wasn't kidding anybody and I knew my desert jaunt would incorporate a lot of walking along with everybody else. Different pressures on the legs and feet from the walking action would cause injury, tiredness and severe blisters if my legs weren't already used to a leg action that was very different from that of running.

★★★

September and October 2011 passed in a whirlwind of physical activity compared to my usual levels.

I wanted to complete the Yorkshireman Off-Road Marathon in September. As a psychological lift, my first marathon since my last at the end of an Ironman triathlon in 2005, it was a means to kick-start my body into a level of exercise it would have to get used to in the remaining months.

Was I properly prepared for it? Not really: four weeks previously I'd completed the pre-marathon obligatory 20 mile run (the distance recognised tongue-in-cheek as the half-way point of a marathon), but that followed the previous week's 18.5 mile run. But that was it for long distance preparation for my first marathon in six years: I had taken it too easy.

And I felt it. With about 4.5 kg in my rucksack a very hilly course across the West Yorkshire moors conspired with an addled, dehydrated brain to ensure I lost my way across a moor for a short period towards the end. I covered instead 28.5 miles rather than the 26.2 I was expecting. This was something I later learnt was a traditional result in the world of off-road running. A slow time was expected using my run/walk strategy but that time was extended by the agony of my cramping legs.

It was a long 6 hours and 29 minutes that I wasn't expecting but I bathed in the feeling of accomplishment from utter exhaustion. I could run a marathon again. It wasn't pretty, but psychologically and physically this gave me a bounce to introduce me to the hard work I'd experience in the coming winter months.

* * *

The off-road events and training runs I completed gathered rapidly: two weeks after the Yorkshireman Off-Road Marathon the 20 miles and 3000 foot of ascent of the In Pendle's Shadow event saw me and my by-now faithful friend my OMM 32 litre rucksack slip and slide across the fields of Lancashire.

It was my second introduction to a LDWA event with its army of volunteers and kindly old gents and ladies, slickly run with a bountiful supply of cake and other goodies at every checkpoint (the best element of a LDWA event).

On one approach to a checkpoint I was running alongside a steep grassy bank, with too many cows in the way, and as I dodged a particularly slothful Friesian I slipped way down the bank, sliding down on my left side through a plentiful supply of wet cow excrement.

Once I stopped I jumped up and thought it best not to wipe myself down of the slop. But this meant I stank.

Onward to the checkpoint, just ahead. The couple of ladies manning a pristine smorgasbord of goodies looked in horror as I approached, a running man ensconced in a bright green jacket with half of it sporting an unfashionable odd dark brown look.

"Oh dear, you look as if you've been in the wars. I don't know if I have anything to help… "

"I slipped in the cow pats." Distracted, I was too busy eyeing the piles of millionaire shortbread.

The kindly old lady um'd and ah'd, desperately wanting to help.

"I don't know if this will do?" She very generously produced a small square of tissue from her sleeve and offered it to me.

I took another look at the left side of my body, covered in a slick of cow slop.

"That's very kind, thank you! Not to worry though!"

A big smile crossed my face as I remembered my Nan, long since departed, and delighted in the knowledge that the Universal Law of Grannies still persisted: that, no matter the circumstances, every Nan and Granny will always have a couple of squares of tissue up her sleeve to vainly try to remove life's mishaps.

I grabbed a couple of millionaire shortbread and bounded on.

★ ★ ★

The following week's event was the Grin 'n Bear It, a hard slog in unseasonably warm weather across the bogs of the Pennines, with a 20 miler the following week.

Two weeks thereafter was the excellent and beautiful scenery of the John O'Gaunts Challenge, a 25 miler with 2,500 feet of total ascent. And the week after that during an 18 miler around the Isle of Lewis on holiday severe winds were stronger than the gravitational force trying to keep me on the ground: I figured it was best to return to the cottage before I disappeared into the lochs.

All of these runs were accompanied with my rucksack, by now packed with about 3-5 kg of weight with towels, bottles of water and other kit. It was a far cry from just a few months ago when I was worried about the ability to exceed 20 miles a week without injury; now, a 30 mile-plus week felt fine. For all of these weeks I stuck to the original plan of not running more than four sessions a week, the mid-week runs being not much more than five or six miles each.

The grim weather of November arrived and with it the decision that now was the time to introduce a concentration on back-to-back runs, considering that was what the Marathon des Sables was largely about. But I didn't want to do this with too much weight just yet: back-to-back runs with too much weight too early would simply bring on injury.

November 2011 was a modest start:

- week 1: 21 miles Saturday followed by 4.1 miles Sunday (6.7 kg rucksack);
- week 2: 4 miles Saturday followed by 22.5 miles Sunday (5.1 kg rucksack);
- week 3: 25 miles (5 kg rucksack).

Feeling tired I took a couple of weeks off.

A mid-December marathon run was completed with 5.5 kg in

the rucksack, increased to 8.9 kg on a 22.5 mile run the following week. At this weight I was now beginning to feel it: I finished with legs I could barely move, a neck I could barely turn and my back muscles aching miserably. My ritual of a cold water bath for my lower body after every long run was though doing a fine job in flushing out the lactic acid and pains, though with the water now at that time of year at 5C it took some resolve to continue with it.

After Christmas I had three months of training left to do. It was critical to keep up the back-to-back runs with a weighted rucksack while at the same time ensuring any chance of injury was kept at bay.

★★★

New Year's Eve 2011 saw a 10 mile run; New Year's Day saw an early start for the 20 mile New Hangover Hike, another LDWA Challenge event I ran with 5.7 kg on my back.

A week later I wanted a challenge. I hadn't yet completed a significant distance of just walking. All of my runs, particularly when carrying a weighted rucksack, included walking breaks of up to a few minutes per mile. But the running action when compared to the walking action are very different. This would find me out in the Marathon des Sables when carrying 10 kg or so, unless I had prepared myself for it mentally and physically.

I wished I could have picked a better day: I woke up early for breakfast and left it to settle for a couple of hours before setting off into the dark, cloudy rains of, weather-wise, a miserable day. With my rucksack packed to the brim with 10.6 kg of kit I wanted to walk around 30 miles without stopping.

I trudged on from home along the Dales Way long distance footpath. The hours passed. Eight hours and 40 minutes later I returned home after 31 miles of non-stop walking. I'd felt freezing cold for the last several hours. Drenched through I had by now suffered a severe case of thigh and testicular chaffing, the last thing I wanted. I found myself in agony with every movement of my legs as drenched lycra shorts and long running tights carved their way into the raw skin of my nether regions. My upper back and neck were in parts numb, in others I felt stabs of pain.

The cold water bath this time was excruciating, so it quickly became a far more pleasant hot bath. I'd met the task and felt a boost of confidence in having walked the distance across some rough country with 10.6 kg. With a five miler after a day's rest followed by a 10 miler, I was pleased with my 46 mile week.

I took a week's rest knowing that, it now being late January, I had just a few weeks of tough back-to-backs to do and the hard training would be over.

★★★

The back-to-backs continued after another week's rest in mid-January:

- week one: 23.1 miles with 5.7 kg Wednesday/14 miles with 11.1 kg Thursday;
- week two: 25 miles with 7.1 kg Thursday/15.1 miles with 9.2 kg Friday;
- week three: 18.5 miles fast march with 10.5 kg Wednesday; 27 miles with 5.5 kg Saturday.

These weeks continued to include other shorter distances for the remainder of the week, for example, an eight mile threshold pace run (that is, on the verge of feeling an all-out pace) with or without a rucksack of up to 9.7 kg, or a five mile faster run without any weight at all.

After that three week cycle I felt I needed to recharge my batteries and took a week off entirely, other than for gentle stretching. For that three week cycle I had exceeded the magic 50 miles a week of running and walking.

★★★

Mid-February 2011. I was now in the final phase of hard training. I was feeling it now and quite often tired, eating larger quantities of food and sleeping longer and deeper. But my weight was dropping off and with it I felt lighter and stronger.

I had also by now entered the Grantham Ultra for the weekend of 10 and 11 March, my final test: a 29 mile run from Cotgrave to Grantham on the Saturday to then get up and do the same route in reverse on the Sunday. 58 miles in two days would be a great test for the demands of the Marathon des Sables. I wanted to fine tune my training in the last few weeks before that event to put in a reasonable show for myself.

But first the final leg of hard training to finish off February and flow into March:

- week 1: 20 miles with 8.5 kg Wednesday/20 miles with 6.6 kg Thursday (50 miles total for the week);
- week 2: 26.2 miles with 6.5 kg Friday/ 5.1 miles with no weight Saturday (40.3 miles total for the week);
- week 3: 23 miles with 11.8 kg Wednesday; day off; 20 miles with 2 kg Friday (49 miles total for the week).

This took me to week 4 which would include my final test, the Grantham Ultra.

The first day felt good: a scenic flat route along the Grantham canal with a variety of competitors, including other MdS entrants, was on a cool spring day. I carried around 6 kg on the first 29 mile leg and finished pleased with my 5 hours and 45 minutes. A thorough stretch before a cold bath plunge did the trick in keeping me relatively discomfort-free for the following day's 29 miles back to Cotgrave with, again, around 6 kg.

There were just two more things to do before bed on the first day: get my compulsory ECG print-out that I would have to hand in when arriving in Morocco and listen to the event organiser, ultra-marathon runner and performance coach Rory Coleman, give tips in his informative evening talk about the MdS.

Getting my ECG test was simple enough: the doctor did his thing and pronounced me alive with no indication on my print-out of any abnormal heart rhythm. This print-out was a compulsory item for the MdS check-in and so I would need to guard this until I got out to Morocco.

Rory's talk was, as expected, useful and entertaining. The guy next to me, Richard (whom would later become one of our tent's occupants), and I swapped training war-stories. Rory did a great job in rousing the room and it was fascinating to hear of other competitors' stories as some weren't there for the MdS at all. One chap had that year's goal as completing an event around Lake Windermere in the summer, the Brathay 10 in 10, completing 10 marathons in 10 days; one or two others were talking about running the dreaded The Spine, "Britain's most brutal race… "

Rory's MdS photos really though did the trick of instilling how grim the MdS could potentially be, delighting in the pictures of a previous year's competitor's feet that, after a few days of sand and oppressive heat, resembled what you'd buy as spare ribs in the local Chinese takeaway.

Our mouths already wide-open from the voyeuristic show of competitors' MdS-battered limbs, Rory warned us:

"Last year, the heat was *unbearable*!! Any ideas what it reached? *56 degrees centigrade*. One of the hottest years on record. Believe me, it's tough."

We had no way of comprehending what that temperature meant or felt like, to be surrounded for hours by an all-enveloping heat. I certainly had no idea at that time but it wouldn't be too long now before I would find out.

★★★

After a fitful night's sleep and a bag of my intended MdS breakfast, powdered milk with cereal (yum! just add water!) it was time to line up to run the 29 miles back to where we started out the day before.

I felt fine through most of it, pacing myself evenly and reminding myself to eat and drink far earlier than normal. It was during the last hour to the finish that I began to feel increasingly weak and sick as the day got hotter and my legs started to cramp.

Finishing in a slower 6 hours 16 minutes I slumped to the floor as cramps got the better of me, as did a bout of nausea. Fortunately I didn't throw up. I took a quick shower and got in the car for the drive home, my legs having carried me 58 miles in two days.

The hard part was over and I felt ready. Sort of.

⋆⋆⋆

I had four weeks left. What to do?

I figured it would be sensible to gently taper down for four weeks and be sure of avoiding injury which, for me, meant no speed training at all. So the Friday after the Grantham Ultra weekend I took a gentle long run of 18 miles with a 14 miler the week after. Other than a few four or five mile runs in-between and in the two weeks before flying out my two years or so of training were finally finished. Stretching and some heat exposure was all else I felt I needed to do, and constantly pack and repack my precious trusty rucksack.

⋆⋆⋆

Heat

The final piece of the jigsaw: how to deal with the Moroccan Sahara's heat.

With temperatures there rising above 50C compared to March temperatures in the UK barely passing 10C I imagined I was going to be roasted alive with a rucksack melting on my back: was there anything I could do to adapt?

I devoured Mike Stroud's chapter entitled 'Marathon of the Sands' in his book *Survival of the Fittest* which goes into great detail about the science of how the human body copes with extremes of heat. It was a wonder absorbing new fascinating facts: the fact that, being a very dry air, the desert would suck moisture away from my skin, being drier than my skin's surface as I sweated. I would need to remember this as signs of sweating would not be a reliable indicator of how hard I was working in the extreme temperatures. I also learnt that as I began to sweat more efficiently my body should, as time wore on, reabsorb most of the salts I really didn't want to lose.

I would not know what each of those phenomena felt like in the chilly UK: as any runner knows, sweat produced on any run in the UK climate, particularly on high humidity summer days, stays as sweat.

Somehow I would have to use other methods in the couple of weeks before I flew out to Morocco to safely have my body get used to an increased core temperature, as far as that was possible. It wasn't critical to do so but I figured any help would be welcome. I'd read that I need only do this for a week to 10 days before reaching Morocco: the human body adapts quickly to changes in heat.

My available choices for getting some heat acclimation were though limited. The latest rage appeared to be an hour or so of Bikram yoga on a regular basis, a constant flow of yoga exercises ideally performed in a room heated to 40C. That option wasn't available to me. Nor was another option: exercising in a heat chamber, considering there were few to be found.

Fortunately I had a Turkish baths near to where I lived and felt that was a realistic possibility. It wasn't perfect as I wouldn't be able to exercise in the rooms where everyone else would be reclined or sat relaxing (and running on the spot in my Speedo swimming briefs would probably cause some alarm). The high humidity in the baths would also be the opposite of what I needed for the desert but I figured that any excessive heat experience would be better than nothing.

I began my heat acclimation in the 13 days prior to flying out to Morocco, using a combination of methods.

I wore a few extra layers on some of my runs: with UK temperatures climbing I could feel myself getting hotter as the runs progressed but I steadfastly refused to remove the woolly hat and three layers under a waterproof jacket as the sun's warmth climbed. At home and with a roaring log fire blazing away for a few hours it felt uncomfortably warm at first to be sat in a big, thick woolly jumper. My wife couldn't comprehend it.

Another good wheeze on a surprisingly warm spring day was to travel on an errand in a very hot car: while most drivers were driving around with the windows down I had mine fully closed… with both the heater and the blower on maximum, wearing a T-shirt and a fleece. I arrived after an hour's drive in a very hot car, flushed and sweating, to the confused looks of passers-by. Hot car journeys were added to the menu of what I could do to build some heat tolerance.

Then came my first of 10 daily trips to the Turkish baths. I went straight into the hottest humid room: 70C. Once I got used to being able to breath again I simply sat there for a full hour. After five minutes I was dripping buckets of sweat that tasted extremely salty, knowing this not because I was licking my armpits but because of the streams of fluid running plentifully down my face. After 45 minutes I started feeling nauseous: I would remember to bring in a 750 millilitre bottle of water to drink for my future sessions.

As the days progressed the one hour sessions became easier. What was noticeable was that on the days when the usual maximum 70C temperature for the room was exceeded, because the boilers were mistakenly left on overnight, a 73C room saw a significantly higher heart rate maximum: between 130 and 138 beats per minute as opposed to a more usual maximum of 112 to 122 beats per minute, despite an increase of just 3C.

For one night during this period my wife and I went to a spa hotel and I continued the heat room experience: an 85C room was unbearable after 15 minutes and even without my heart rate monitor onboard I could tell from how I was feeling that my body wasn't thanking me for it.

What this showed was that I'd need to be wary of significantly higher temperatures while exercising strenuously in the desert: my heart rate wouldn't cope and I'd struggle to dissipate any overheating.

At the end of my heat acclimation period, the day before I travelled to Gatwick for my overnight stay prior to flying out, I had though noticed some interesting changes.

It took a longer period of time towards the end of the sessions when compared with the first couple for me to end up sweating profusely: in the first session this took five minutes; in the last session it took around 11 minutes. I also noticed that the taste of salts in my sweat was significantly reduced by the final session when compared to the bitter taste experienced in the first session. Finally both the average and maximum heart rates, after having peaked at days 5 and 6, dropped off thereafter despite by then my having introduced very light exercise stretches.

I'm no scientist, but I figured that these efforts to try and raise and get used to a higher temperature would have a positive effect, if only psychologically.

3

Arrival

Wednesday 4 April 2012

I carried out a final pack and repack, for the umpteenth time over the last few weeks. I managed to get it all in the rucksack, packed away neatly, and hadn't seemingly missed anything: hopefully. I went for a haircut first thing: a number 1 back and sides and a number 2 top as I couldn't be doing with too much hair on a sweaty head. I met my wife for lunch as it would be the last I'd see of her for over a week. With neither of us knowing what to expect in the coming days she was upset as I was leaving and I was starting to feel the same.

I wasted a little time at the rail station as my excitement began to build before my 14.15 train would depart for London: to Starbucks for a hot chocolate, to Sainsbury's for a large bottle of water. I knew I should keep my fluids topped up as often as I could.

I finished reading Richard Askwith's *Feet in the Clouds* during the quick journey down, which soon passed uneventfully as I contemplated what lay ahead. A quick Tube trip took me across to London Victoria, accompanied by many strange looks at my rucksack complete with a rolled up British flag tucked in the back. I finally arrived at the hotel to unpack and move all my critical kit to my rucksack: that would be coming with me on the plane.

A large pizza was necessary for dinner. I aimlessly watched TV while sorting my feet out to try and reduce blister risk, made a few changes to my rucksack content and then it was to bed for a good night's sleep.

Thursday 5 April 2012

It was another night in which I slept fitfully, worrying about waking up in time to get on the plane to Morocco... although with a departure time of 12 pm that was never going to be a problem.

Such was the anxiety that three years of training and meticulously planning for an event which simply required me to get on a plane by a pre-determined time created.

Although I woke up at 6.15 I dozed until 7.30, despite desperately trying to get to sleep again but the endless whirl of checks and double-checks put paid to that: had I packed everything? have I drunk enough so far? did I bring my passport? will my size-11 trainers with seemingly flimsy gaiters do the job? just how hot will it feel and will I cope? will I finish?

I groggily meandered down to breakfast. Ashley (a fellow MdS entrant whom I'd met through an ultra-running website) and I introduced ourselves after a gradual process of elimination having applied the laws of MdS-entrant identification and excluded pretty much the rest of the breakfast room's occupants. Slim? Appearing physically fit with a short haircut? Winter-tanned complexion from running for hours in the cold and the wind? Yep: there stands another nutter.

We nervously and excitedly chatted about the MdS over breakfast, as you'd expect. I think we both appreciated the chance to talk face-to-face with another person who was actually doing the MdS rather than a long-suffering spouse, friend or work colleague who had put up with MdS-chat for far too long.

It was immediately obvious that Ashley was no stranger to the demands of training and racing long distances, a strong though slight, toned middle-aged chap with the weathered complexion of endless hours running around his training ground of the Snowdonian mountains; indeed, Ashley's first ultra was the gruelling Tour de Mont Blanc in 2005, an event which nowadays requires points accrued from completing other races in order simply to enter it.

Returning to my room I had my penultimate shower and shave before I would abstain for seven days and yet again checked and repacked my small suitcase and rucksack. Meeting up with Ashley we boarded the free bus for the short distance to Gatwick South Terminal.

We very quickly identified the MdS crowd and I wondered how this gaggle appeared to the moving throng of MdS-outsiders: aside from a few MdS veterans, a group of slightly nervous-looking men and women, clutching a small suitcase and equally small rucksack, some of which had seen better days with a variety of DIY-modifications, looking hungry and lean with (predominantly) military-style haircuts. Where were they going? Why did they all have a suitcase and a rucksack with DIY adjustments? Few would have twigged.

A quick check-in and onwards through to Departures, via a strictly-speaking illegal purchase of some Moroccan dirhams at the foreign exchange. The feeling of strong camaraderie was already palpable as a common purpose united the gaggle in common conversation: there can be few instances where complete strangers can strike up a conversation or exchange banter or ask questions without being ignored or viewed suspiciously.

I bumped into Richard (whom I met at the Grantham Ultra Q&A evening) and along with Ashley aimed for the pub to pass the time. It was then that Richard and I learnt of Ashley's slight aversion to flying: we both wondered at Ashley's solution to this in downing several strong alcoholic beverages with seemingly very little effect… and were mystified as to how Ashley could be an ultra-runner when he also confessed to having a heavy nicotine habit. Inevitably we swapped training tales and kit stories, measuring up each other's methods and choices, quietly wondering if more grammes could be shaved off the weight of our rucksacks.

I'd already cut off every label, spare buckle, strap and ditched all packaging but it didn't stop the question... *What else*?!

On the way to finally boarding the plane I realised that I would need something to read so, with little time left as the queue started to board, I jogged back to WH Smith to buy a book... only to realise when I left the store that I'd previously read it... so I jogged back to exchange it... and then jogged back to the boarding queue. I was needlessly anxious about missing my flight and had visions of pressing my face up against the glass window of the jet bridge, banging my fists in panicked silent desperation as the Monarch flight taxied down the runway and soared off without me. *Relax... calm down... walk...*

There was a real buzz on boarding as lots of excited people introduced themselves giddily to others out to achieve exactly the same goal. There was a sense of trepidation and excitement, laughter amongst some earnest conversations as the collective thought was one of "*We're finally on our way, after all this time*!"

I sat next to and introduced myself to Mark, a jovial gent of strength from Cornwall and by the end of the 3.5 hour flight myself, Ashley and Mark had become three of our required tent of eight. Making up a tent of eight was one of the first tasks for competitors to resolve by the time we would arrive at the first day's bivouac and Mark already had our fourth tent mate lined up, Wayne, sat a few rows down the plane.

I don't think I've ever known a flight to pass so quickly. I tried to catch up on some sleep, nigh impossible on a plane at the best of times, so instead read a little and chatted with Mark and Ashley over the usual stuff: tales of our hardest training runs, the weight of our rucksacks (envious *oohs* and *aahs* at mine), food choices and whether we thought a particular piece of kit was worth bothering with. Brushing your teeth, or not? Gone overboard on the toilet roll? Or just a few squares?

In seemingly no time at all since having left Gatwick the plane was nearing the Sahara desert outpost town of Ouarzazate. What had been a noisy bubbling plane of excited conversation for three hours fell almost completely silent as we all took in the majestic awe-inspiring views of the Atlas Mountains, snow-covered higher peaks giving way to a deceptively flat planet of arid red desert and treacherous rocky mountains. Excited conversation lapsed into infrequent, barely audible murmurs.

We landed into balmy late afternoon temperatures of 20C that felt a lot cooler in the breeze. I'd recalled reading somewhere that getting to grips with the MdS is in part also about getting to grips with the concept of queuing a lot and our first instance of this was the immigration queue: albeit we were barely a queue of 200 people it took me 75 minutes to get through once in the warm immigration building with plenty of others queuing behind me. This wasn't helped by a sudden down-tools of the two immigration guards: disappearing regularly for a random 10 minutes for an apparent fag break was the norm.

Still, more introductions and general chit-chat passed the time. As did observing what appeared to be Moroccan security people stood around us with no apparent purpose other than to look menacing at border control: look-alikes with dark hair, moustaches, menacing looks, black polo-neck jumpers with dark leather-elbow patched jackets. They just stood around looking menacing for a while until apparent boredom saw them melt away, probably for a fag break, or to look menacing elsewhere.

The training story of a Yorkshireman in front of us was an inspiration: with little time to train due to shift work he had been running up and down steep forested hills around his neighbourhood in the depths of winter at around midnight wearing a head torch, only to get up a few hours later for his next shift. Proving the point that where there's the will to train for the MdS, there is a way…

Once through Immigration a coach was waiting to take the

next batch of us the very short drive to the Berbere Palace Hotel. Apparently a 5-star facility the UK contingent always got the best hotel in Ouarzazate and this year was no exception. Allegedly, to the annoyance of the French.

After checking in and dumping our few worldly goods in our rooms it was a short few steps across the road to the shop for bottled water: must keep the water works flowing. And the shop owners weren't missing a trick: crate upon crate of bottled water was piled up high as an offering to this year's MdS contingent.

We met Mark and Wayne and wandered to the nearby cashpoint and back, now a confirmed group of four for our tent. We started to appreciate how hot it could get: an early evening short walk saw us sweating freely.

The dinner buffet was a hoot of excitable chat. Richard appeared with another tent mate, Dean, and now we were six; Mark popped off and introduced two others: Paul and Tony. Mission accomplished: we now had a tent of eight!

Few spent too long in the bar after gorging on food: most seemed too tired and wanted to eke out as many quality hours of sleep as possible before hitting the desert. We went back to our rooms for the repacking ritual: it was an early start in the morning and no-one was that keen on having to mess around too much doing that in the desert.

4

Bivouac

Friday 6 April 2012

I hadn't slept properly for a few nights by now, the result of a mixture of excitement and nerves that conspired with the endless chatter in my head that was checking and double-checking if I'd packed everything and whether I had all the correct bits of paperwork. The nightmare was of having got this far after some three years and having forgotten some vital piece of paper or equipment. I just wanted to get out into the desert and hand in my baggage, to be left with the simplicity of nothing but my small rucksack and the clothes I stood in.

Having woken up and fallen asleep several times I finally woke up before the alarm at 6.15 am. Ashley went off for breakfast while I took care over what would be my last shave and shower for 7 days and then packed up.

Once Ashley was back I headed for the bustling breakfast room, by now fully wide awake along with everybody else, nervously laughing and chatting away. I wanted to keep the risk of diarrhoea and vomiting down so I chose what I thought would be a simple but filling breakfast: a few pastries, a sealed pot of natural yoghurt and an omelette. The eggs later proved to be a bad choice.

Ready and checked out by 8 am, as required by the detailed printed instructions we'd been given the day before, most of our tent crew converged in the lobby: me, Ashley, Wayne, Mark, Tony and Paul. Richard and Dean were already sunning themselves outside, grinning away, and joined us at the bivouac later.

Emerging outside and wincing in the strong bright light a sea of MdS entrants had already taken up most of the street. The temperature steadily and notably climbed: having not long emerged from several months of a cold, dark, freezing UK it felt both odd and rejuvenating to feel so warm in blazing sunshine so early in the morning.

Gradually we all piled onto the coaches and finally set off in convoy, stopping briefly just outside Ouarzazate for a human chain of MdS volunteers to load up the coaches with a supply of water and packed lunches. I sat next to Tom and exchanged MdS talk but the journey was mostly a quiet murmur of conversation as most of us sat in our own thoughts contemplating what lay ahead, or fell asleep.

After some time the French *controlleur* accompanying us began handing out the booklet we'd been dying to see: the official MdS roadbook for 2012, the detailed (well, sketchy…) instructions of how we would get from one checkpoint to another for each stage. Almost all firstly turned to the pages dealing with Stage 4 to confirm what distance we would have to run for the fear-inducing long stage: 50.9 miles. After getting over that we wondered how easy it would be in practice to follow the sketch maps that made no attempt to convey scale: detail was absent from very basic, pen-drawn pictures. Still, it was all part of the challenge.

The coach journey took its time meandering and forever descending along mountain and desert roads as we absorbed a real sense of the Moroccan landscape. The scenery was spectacular: steep, dark, rocky mountains gave way to endless desert plains, dotted with the odd oasis of palm trees and a little greenery, with miles of uninterrupted views: not a building in sight and only a rare glimpse of other vehicles. It was the first time I had a real sense of space: there can be few places in the world where views of sky, land and horizon can be so vast and uninterrupted.

Eventually the coaches stopped for a very welcome 5 minute "relief" break: the message had finally reached the drivers that a few hundred men and women had been knocking back mineral water for the last couple of hours and many were by now desperate. Some unspoken and unwritten rule saw the men charge off to the right atop a stony bank for a urinating endurance competition while the women charged off to the left to find some scrub to hide behind. A short while later a longer 45 minute lunch stop was very welcome to stretch out cramped legs in the desert plain stretching out in the shadow of the mountains: the French fayre of bread, cheese and a few other edible items tasted pretty good and were more than adequate. Having markedly descended over the last few hours from the land height of Ouarzazate the temperature in this windless stopping place began to cause concern.

At about this point I really started to feel unwell: I figured having the omelette at breakfast was the culprit. Back on the coach after lunch I knew a dicky tummy was approaching but it didn't seem too bad so far. As we'd left Ouarzazate by 9.30 am and we'd been informed the journey to the bivouac was about 3.5 hours I figured I could easily hold on for another hour.

Unfortunately, French time-keeping seemed to have been brought along with a French passion for queuing and the French *controlleur* riding with us on the coach just gave a traditional Gallic shrug when asked, like a child: "How much longer?"

"Ah don no… Shood be there now! Mare be coople urs?!"

"Oh well," I thought, "on such a modern coach there'll be a toilet at the back." I turned to look and saw rows of people on seats and… no toilet.

Damn.

It was another 2 hours that must count as some of the longest and most uncomfortable in my life. I was transported back to unconscious memories of childhood as all the repressed fears of toileting came back: will I make it in time? what if I soil my pants?

can I hold it in? can I really ask this thundering convoy of 6 coaches to stop in the middle of a huge empty desert plain for just one person to get off and seek refuge behind... oh no! there's no refuge anywhere! I'm in the middle of a desert!

Horrors filled my mind of before long *really* having to insist that the coach be stopped, of sprinting out onto a sandy plain with absolutely no natural cover to evacuate my bowels in front of a few hundred open-mouthed and horrified onlookers staring out the windows of the coaches in my direction. I'd have to leave the race immediately in shame and return to the UK, forever known as That Guy Who Did A Dump In Full View of 6 Coaches.

As the pain of my bowels increased to quite great proportions I kept looking ahead up the road to see any sign of a tree or significant bush... Nothing. Tom, sat next to me, asked if I was OK as I began breaking out in a feverish sweat, holding my stomach: "Desperately need the toilet... " I replied. Tom started looking very concerned, perhaps in fear I may explode everywhere.

Finally, some 5 hours (not the intended 3.5) or more since leaving Ouarzazate the coaches turned off the smooth tarmac road and bounced along a badly rutted track. *At last!* I thought. Can't be much longer now.

The rutted track seemed to last quite a while though and the coach finally came to a stop where open-topped cattle trucks awaited the first couple of loads of competitors to take them the rest of the distance of about a mile to the bivouac.

The minute the coach started to pull up I rushed to the front with one of my precious rations of toilet paper, asking the *controlleur* to wait for me as I desperately needed the toilet. He looked alarmed as I did a weird lumbering-cum-wobble sprint to hide at the back of a disused building, hoping the gang of congregating Moroccan kids wouldn't follow me, and relieved the pain messily. Oh, the relief... I felt very guilty though for sullying the event's environmental credentials by having to also leave my cotton boxer shorts behind with my toilet paper. Still, at least they were biodegradable.

But I needn't have been so concerned about this episode: after the first couple of stages of the MdS it became *de rigueur* to be vomiting and crapping all over the place in front of an audience, whether in the field or at the back of the bivouac.

Still with a dodgy stomach I returned more relaxed to the coach drop-off area to collect my suitcase and rucksack until the panic of realisation set in that I'd left my jumper and, more importantly, my Frillneck sunhat on the coach… and the coach had already left.

This wasn't really going to plan.

I didn't fancy trying to run for 7 days across the Sahara without vital head protection: that would be disastrous, and it wasn't as if competitors were arriving with spare sunhats. The *controlleur* said he'd checked and nothing was left behind; Ashley had very kindly waited for me and said he'd seen someone take my stuff off the coach. I'd have to go searching for it once at the bivouac. My head was already starting to boil in the hot sun and I knew I'd feel my life was forever complete once I was reunited with my sunhat.

The open-topped cattle trucks had by now left and Moroccan army trucks staffed by gruff Moroccan Army personnel had arrived for their next run. Ashley and I opted for the truck with its tarpaulin left on in some unconscious awareness that this was preferable to those trucks with the tarpaulin removed. A wise decision, as it turned out.

Truck full we now got going: think of riding a terrifying rollercoaster without wearing a harness.

The drivers (mustachioed look-alikes again) were on a mission, to deliver their cargo in the quickest possible time, as they sped across the undulating, rocky plain: the 10 or so of us in the back bounced around violently in the dust clouds, the odd yelp of pain signalling coccyx or bony limb meeting the floor of the truck, for a good 10 minutes before arriving at the bivouac. The truck's tarpaulin had largely protected us from the sand clouds, a benefit the coughing and spluttering occupants in the trucks we overtook didn't have.

We were met by the sight of a sea of black "tents" arranged in two horseshoe shapes, one horseshoe sitting in the concave of the other. The outer horseshoe contained mostly the British sector of the competitors' bivouac.

"Tents" is, though, rather a grand term: these were basic Berber tents, a large black sheet of heavy cotton canvas (variously perforated to enhance that genuine sand storm experience) supported by wooden poles in the four corners and the front- and back-middle, and left open to the elements front and back. We later found though it was easy enough in a sand storm to collapse the poles in the middle to try and close off the outside world, though this didn't prevent the inside of the tent becoming a mist, nor did it prevent scratched eyes and a heaving chest, as fine sand particles thickly penetrated the ageing canvas.

It was only a short walk from the truck to the British sector of the competitors' bivouac, dragging my cumbersome small suitcase across the sand, where we found Mark, Wayne, Tony and Paul already installed and looking thoroughly relaxed, reclining on their sleeping bags and contemplating the huge desert views.

I liked the look of that but first I wanted to finally rearrange my suitcase into neat compacted piles of stuff I wouldn't need for seven days: I would then have less to do in the morning before handing it all in. Mark was very impressed with my housekeeping and offered to pay me 10 Moroccan Dirhams to do his. As this amounted to about £1 I politely declined.

Before long I was reunited with my top and sunhat that I'd left on the coach; Tom had been a gent and handed it to a *controlleur* who had now come to find me. A massive relief...

The rest of the day was fast passing; by 7 pm it would be dark. Tonight would be the only night we could sleep under canvas and get some idea of what sleeping arrangements worked (what night-time clothing to wear? do I use a pillow or not?) before we were left with the very basics after check-in the next day.

★★★

Some more form filling passed the time and I was finished with what I had to do. A second trip to the toilet used a second precious ration of my week's toilet roll and gloves but this wasn't as violent as earlier. I took an Immodium out of my ration to try and finish it off: I'd obviously eaten something disagreeable rather than having caught a bad illness… notably Tony had also contracted the trots having also had eggs in the morning at the hotel. Dehydration and stomach sickness wasn't really what we needed barely a day before we were about to run across the desert for 153 miles.

By this point we had found out what the rolled tube of brown plastic left in the middle of the tent was for. The combined intelligence of 8 men in this particular tent, which had first thought this tube was some kind of flare or receptacle for sending letters home in the event of death, couldn't work out what this tube was: we only found out by asking a somewhat bemused-looking MdS representative who confirmed this was our roll of plastic bags for the toilet… and to think we were soon to be let loose and left to our own devices to run across the desert…

The representative, laughing, also assured us we would get more bags on a daily basis when we became very concerned there were only about 5 bags for 8 blokes… and I was about to use one of them.

In previous years, by some accounts, the toilet provisions had been pretty disastrous: reports were plentiful of the inside of the basic toilet "cubicle" resembling the aftermath of a couple of hundred pigeons having been cooped up for a day. It wasn't a surprise that diarrhoea and vomiting consequently would take hold across the camp: we needed to remain vigilant. Catching this could easily put paid to any chances of finishing the race.

So originally my plan, to keep sickness away, was to abandon the official toilets and go *en plein air*. It seemed a shame though in the circumstances to not take advantage of the pristine toilet cubicles that were calling to me in the sunshine like the Sirens of Greek mythology not 50 metres from the back of the good ship Tent 78. So I bravely agreed to be the first in the tent to try them out.

It was all very civil really which, when combined with my routine, did much to keep toilet problems minimal for most of the week.

A MdS toilet routine: that's what a few years of thinking about and preparing for the race does to you: every tiny detail is considered. The last thing I wanted was to fail to complete this race because of incapacitating vomiting or diarrhoea. I was particularly proud of my well-thought out toilet routine.

First installed in the 2011 race, these toilets were designed by the Norwegian army. Four pieces of six foot rectangular tarpaulin formed the four sides of the "cubicle", the one furthest and facing away from the bivouac being the "door". Two or three of these cubicles were attached together, allowing for a tad too up-close shared appreciation of bodily functions. The Norwegian-designed "toilet" itself resembled a small square plastic picnic table which sits on its legs with a large hole cut out of the square top. Presented with this comforting picture so begins the routine.

Having left the tent with one of my 8 allotted packets of toilet materials I would enter the tent with my upper arm, sweeping aside the heavy tarpaulin. My packet of materials safely tucked under my arm (to avoid ground contamination… you don't want to know) the brown plastic bag is opened and, like a bin liner to a bin, is fitted around the square (note: *very carefully*… the hands are not to touch any part of this plastic "toilet" as part of the routine).

Sit: it is fine at this point to use both hands to drop one's garments as the packet of materials remains tucked under the arm. Open the packet. Place one blue latex glove upon the right hand. Try not to pee first: the weight of the pee in the bag combined with an unexpected movement on the plastic "toilet" could see the brown plastic bag on which one is sat easily slip off and fall to the sandy ground, inviting hygiene predicaments. *Only using this blue latex hand* the toilet ration paper may be accessed from the plastic bag to clean up. Once done, unfurl the blue latex glove using its lower most section with the other hand, turning it inside out. Stand. Drop the glove and the empty packet into the brown plastic bag. Gently unfurl the brown plastic bag.

After one's doings, the bag is carefully peeled off from the square, absolutely not dropped, tied up and deposited into the black bin on exiting the cubicle (perhaps after giving a "*Bonjour!*" to the occupant next door, visible through the large gaps in the tarpaulin). With the clean non-latex hand access the bottle of alcohol hand gel; open; apply liberally to hands.

Voila!

I didn't suffer (much, badly, really, sort of...) in the way of vomiting or diarrhoea all week.

★★★

Back at the tent it was great fun sharing the jokes and we'd all quickly built a rapport. Having sorted the majority of my kit I then wallowed in relaxation in the shade of the tent and a cooler sun to write up my diary. As the sun descended and a light breeze rose it became quite cool very quickly; it didn't take much of a stronger breeze for dust clouds to leave a fine powdery sand settling on everything. At first we were all brushing it off and shaking down our kit and clothes vigorously; after a couple of days and once the race got under way we lacked the energy or inclination to keep doing this in all but the strongest of storms.

By 7 pm it was pitch black, the only lighting coming from some small bonfires lit by competitors outside their tents using gathered scrub, or the few artificial lights about half a mile away at the official canteen area.

We all wandered over to join the long dinner queues to collect some hot food and sit cramped on the floor and squeezed up against neighbours around a round table to chat and eat. Before I came out to Morocco and again thinking of keeping diarrhoea and vomiting at bay I'd thought of bringing out extra food to cook for myself rather than join in the communal canteen but finally decided this would be anti-social and probably unnecessary: it was highly unlikely that our French hosts would allow standards which brought on widespread illness. It was great to sit around chatting about the MdS and our plans, adding to the tent camaraderie; the hygiene standards of the canteen and food were high so I needn't have had any concerns there.

The canteen area was a little cramped and, with most of us having been running for years to get this far, we lacked the flexibility to sit comfortably for too long on the matted floor on our knees or cross-legged. With head torches on we meandered our way back to Tent 78 to stumble around in the dark to sort out our sleeping kit (in amongst constant urinating from having drunk so much water). I remember standing around in the impossibly bright moonlight chatting with Rich, Ashley and Dean, nerves a-plenty and an eerie silence descending around the bivouac.

By 8.30 pm it was bed time as there was nothing else to do: reading or whatever by our head torches would be wasting battery life we might need on the dreaded overnight Stage 4. I rolled out my mat and sleeping bag and climbed in wearing my planned night wear: a looser pair of lightweight shorts (to allow the nether regions to breath once back at camp after a hard day's effort) and my buff for a hat: it was already quite chilly but once cocooned in my Mammut Ajungilak sleeping bag I felt a lot warmer.

In amongst Mark trumping like a true champion I recounted my journey of terror on the coach journey to get out here. In a true no-nonsense Cumbrian accent Wayne simply uttered quietly:

"That's why I took two Immodium before I got on the coach, and I'll be taking two going back."

Tent 78 went quiet momentarily to contemplate and digest this obvious MdS wisdom.

★★★

Saturday 7 April

Yet again I had another poor night's sleep. I was very aware that I'd have to try and catch up later that day (which was unlikely) or get a good night's sleep tonight before the start of the race tomorrow (also unlikely). The compounded effect of a lack of sleep was later to prove interesting on the overnight Stage 4.

Last night was supposed to be a test to see what sleeping arrangements worked. I was quite comfortable getting into my sleeping bag and dozing off but I found myself too hot and sweating by 11 pm as my sleeping bag clung like cling-film. I completely unzipped my bag and took off my Buff... only to find I was freezing cold at 1 am and went hunting for my T-shirt in my rucksack... by which time Ashley's snoring to my right resembled a series of bombs going off... and on Ashley's breathing out Mark's snoring to my left ensured a continuous threshold of noise.

I was being driven mad! They probably felt the same though when I kept waking up to hunt for my discarded T-shirt. Eventually I got to sleep but repeated a cycle of waking up feeling too hot then falling asleep only to awake shivering and frozen, hunting again for my discarded T-shirt as the desert temperature dropped significantly around 4 am. I was also struggling to get comfy on my thin Thermarest (I don't think I'd inflated it correctly): it was barely wider than my shoulders so any movement to turn on my side saw me finding the blanketed, hard stony ground. Not inflating it so much on subsequent nights seemed to help a little, or maybe I was simply too exhausted to notice or care.

What I also found was that as it got colder through the night in the open tent (in a part of the desert where temperatures can drop to as low as 2-3C) the tiniest gap in the top of my sleeping bag meant the cold air sucked any warmth out rapidly, leaving cold spots and draughts working their way up and around my increasingly shivering body. I was constantly fiddling with the top of my sleeping bag to adjust my temperature. I kept rolling off my mat as I moved to get comfortable, the Thermarest noisily crinkling away like a massive inflated crisp packet, and every time I did I found patches of cold, rocky ground jarring me from semi-sleep.

Finally Earth began to wake as did the rest of the tent as the pitch black gave way to a dull and then beautifully bright sunny morning. It was 6.10 am.

"Well that was a shit night's sleep!" said Rich with his trademark huge grin and a laugh. I wasn't the only one then! Like a bunch of old washer women various jocular complaints went around the tent:

"Who the hell's snoring was that?!"

"Who kept fiddling around in their rucksack all night?"

Oops, that might have been me.

It took a short while longer for the sun's warmth to remove the ambient chill and during that time I refused to get out of what was finally a comfortably warm sleeping bag. At about 7 am I ambled slowly over to the queue in the centre of the bivouac horseshoe to collect my day's ration of water bottles. Today was to be the first day of getting used to water rationing, the previous day being a free-for-all: this 3 litres was to include my drinking (of which there'd be plenty), cooking (of which there'd be little as breakfast, lunch and dinner would be supplied by the organisers) and washing (of which there'd just be cleaning my teeth in the morning: for the evening and rest of the week I'd be using spearmint chewing gum to do the job).

Back at the tent and before breakfast I began to get my suitcase in order, for the last time, having made some decisions by now on kit and what I'd send back to the hotel after our first night in the bivouac; a few of us wandered over to the canteen area for a simple but plentiful meal.

It was to be a long day of waiting around and doing very little. At the time I think we were all itching to get going, becoming tired and restless of the queues and administration. Looking back now I recognise the administration day was in fact quite special: there can be few moments in life as an adult with responsibilities where there is the opportunity to simply lie back on a hot sunny day, encumbered by nothing more than the clothes on one's back and a small rucksack, admire some spectacular natural views, and… simply… do… nothing…

Returning to the tent from breakfast I went into administration mode: I needed to get my suitcase back to the hotel and my rucksack content finalised. As part of this process I figured that, by the time I got back to the hotel after the race (assuming I finished it) I'd be in a pretty run-down state and possibly not thinking straight: packing decisions now would save some stress and time later.

So I completely unpacked my suitcase and repacked it tightly to ensure maximum space, folding into tight rolls any clothes that would simply be going back to the UK to be washed while folding neatly everything else I'd need to change into once back at the hotel.

I needed to ensure I had everything I would need for the next 7 days so I also completely unpacked my rucksack and, day-by-day, ensured I put back in what I knew I would need against the list I'd brought with me. Anything else went back into my suitcase; for

example, I'd decided against taking two pairs of outer
pair of Thorlos went back to the hotel in the suitcase.

After the suitcase and rucksack process I felt so muc
But only an hour had passed since coming back from break

★★★

Suddenly... excitement!

"Guys, a camel spider."

Wayne was stood outside the tent pointing to the ground. He seemed particularly deadpan and calm about this, which seemed odd: seeing a camel spider in the desert was, after all, one of the main reasons for coming out to race the MdS and a main potential source of excitement.

A few of us leapt up from our relaxed positions in the tent in eager anticipation while keeping a respectful distance from this monster of the desert.

"Is that it?!"

We were singularly unimpressed and now understood Wayne's lack of initial panic. The camel spider was barely visible, cleverly camouflaged (being seemingly transparent) against the sand. Our disappointment was with its size. But at about 2 inches long and looking to be capable of a nasty bite we still didn't want it anywhere near us: we did all we could to shoo it away to Tent 77 next door.

It must have been around 9.30 am by now... It seemed to take an age to get to 10 am and for the first few of Tent 78 to amble over to Control to pass the compulsory checks and drop off their suitcases. Sat in the shade I was feeling chilly with goosebumps on my legs. Blocks of 5 minutes seemed like blocks of an hour. I made a last-minute decision: I decided I didn't need the headstrap for my Adidas Evil Eye sunglasses so in the suitcase they went. A combination of my Buff, Frillneck and sunglasses should deal adequately with any sandstorms.

… lot, absorbed some warmth from the
… ot at 11.30 am, concerned at whether
… ne as arranged at 11 am: I'd run out
… it talking to her as the frightening
… versation early, so I didn't know
… y been in the desert for two days
… emplate and I was becoming aware of a
… se of consciousness about what was important in

Still tinkering with my kit I had a surprise call from my wife. The family had just finished an Easter egg hunt. It was lovely to catch up. I gave details about the MdS videos released onto YouTube at 7 pm each night. She started getting upset, not having a clue about what life would be like out here for a week; I tried not to get upset, a long way from home and its creature comforts without much idea myself of what was going to happen over the next few days. I said I'd try and email from tomorrow when the email tent should be set up. I really missed her already.

⋆⋆⋆

At last, more queuing time!

I strolled over at 11.15 am to queue outside the tent complex for the compulsory checks. It took probably a good half hour standing in an increasingly hot sun before refuge was given by the dark cover of the tents. As I was wearing my MdS race kit of running shorts, long-sleeved top and hat it was my legs that were starting to burn as I hadn't yet put sunscreen on: my week's ration didn't allow for sunscreen before Stage 1 of the race. I was also already getting a strong thumping headache despite having drunk plenty of water.

Quickly it all became quite serious; the banter and relaxation of the last couple of days temporarily abated.

Having attached a luggage label the Berbers swiftly took my small suitcase and let it join the mountain of others in the luggage compound. At the tent complex entrance I gave my name and was given two race numbers; I handed in some forms and collected a bag of salt tablets (without being given any instructions on their use, other than the barked order "You must take these!") and my distress flare, about the size of a large family-pack tube of fruit pastilles; I was asked the total weight of my food, the total amount of calories it contained and the weight of my rucksack: in response to each of these questions I showed them a printed sheet with all the detail but on showing it they seemed satisfied I'd done a thorough job and quickly moved me on. A couple of competitors ahead of me, mid- to back-packers like myself, had though been selected for a more thorough rucksack-emptying inspection.

The race doctors gave a cursory look at my ECG printout and medical certificate (along with some comment about so many competitors not speaking French) and I then emerged from the dark, minutes after I'd entered, blinking into a strong sun. Another official explained to me the strict rules for attaching one's race numbers while another was having a minor remonstration with an American competitor who didn't want to play by those rules (after the race that competitor told me he'd been selected for special kit spot checks during several of the race stages, in revenge he thought).

And that was it. All that time planning and testing my kit since 2009, packing and unpacking, worrying about the ECG examination, worrying whether I'd get away with just having 700 calories for the last day Stage 6, about which the rules were unclear… all done.

Ambling slowly back to Tent 78 I began to feel a huge sense of relief and freedom as it dawned on me that what I was wearing and what was in my 32 litre rucksack on my back was my whole world for a week. Walking back to my tent in awe of the vast open skies and endless miles of desert ending in distant *jebels* affirmed for me that entering this race and training and thinking about little else for almost 3 years was worth every minute and every penny. As with much of my MdS experience, I remember this short walk as vividly as if it were yesterday.

★★★

On my amble back to the tent I bumped into Rory Coleman (for whom this year's MdS would be his ninth) and his partner Jen Salter, whom I met on their Grantham Ultra race weekend.

Jen commented that the measuring scales were way off (it had measured their rucksacks at something ridiculously low) and pointed over to an administration tent where earnest-looking competitors stood looking at their rucksacks hanging off a chain, hands on their chins nodding sagely. I decided to pass some time and wander over so I too could look earnest and sage. Having weighed my race-weight rucksack before I left the UK at 8.6 kg I was interested to see what these "official" scales would measure. I knew straight away that my rucksack really wasn't 5.5 kg… I could but dream, albeit even this weight would be below the race's minimum rucksack weight of 6.5 kg.

After dropping off my worldly belongings at the tent a few of us took a light lunch at the canteen. We pitied those standing in what was now a far longer queue for the Control tent, some visibly uncomfortable in what was now a very strong lunchtime sun. Most of us were by now starting to complain of strong headaches in the dry desert heat, and this despite having drunk plenty; there were very few relieving breezes throughout the day. There was also no doubt about it: it was so very hot. The rest of the day was about rest and doing as little as possible to conserve energy and hydration.

Back at the tent we had hours to kill and inevitably we all started talking about why we were doing this event. Attempting to cover over 150 miles on foot in seven days across one of the Earth's most inhospitable deserts is, after all, beyond the realms of normality. For most of us the challenge was about completing something so different and off-the-wall it would stand out forever as one of life's highlights against the white noise of 9-to-5.

Paul was a self-confessed non-runner, preferring cricket, and had hit upon the MdS as simply a different fitness challenge. For a self-confessed non-runner he turned out to be an incredibly efficient and fast one, despite starting out with a rucksack weight of over 11 kg.

During the afternoon it emerged that Tony had completed the MdS last year and simply decided three months ago to come back and have another go. On this news an awed silence swept the tent as all eyes turned to Tony, who had instantly become a god in Tent 78: he was now the father of knowledge on all that is MdS. Although Tony was sadly not to stay with us for much longer he was very generous in the advice he gave.

Mark was no stranger to keeping fit and wanted to complete one of the world's toughest challenges. Mark had already become the glue of Tent 78, admonishing negativity and was always the first to try and get back on track any one of us who found themselves in a poor state in the coming days. He had some great comments when I was explaining why I was doing this race, some of which changed my thinking once I was back home in the UK. He also had a great sense of humour and specialised in fantastic gagging simulations while trying to eat rehydrated freeze-dried meals.

For Ashley the MdS was another event to tick off the list, having already completed the gruelling Tour de Mont Blanc. Ashley could be a very interesting subject for sport science: in between taking regular cigarette breaks during the afternoon he asked us all to just ignore him if we found him collapsed while running. He explained that after running about 20 miles, like clockwork, his body simply seemed to pack up and collapse as he flopped to the ground, but after a few minutes he'd be up again bright as a button and off he'd continue to complete the race. We were on strict instructions not to set off his distress flare if we found him like this. Who were we to argue with someone who regularly ran up and down Mount Snowdon for training?

Nothing seemed to faze Rich and Dean nor dim their almost permanent grins and laughs: you got the impression you could send them off for a 100 mile run and they'd still come back laughing and grinning. I later learnt that Dean had previously spent time travelling the world climbing and naming as-yet-unnamed virgin mountains in distant lands.

Finally Wayne, The Green Giant simply by virtue of being tall and his race kit consisting of a distinctive green Macmillan Cancer Support T-shirt on top of fetching white leggings and top. Wayne was raising money for Macmillan Cancer Support, spurred on by the loss of his grandmother recently. With a great sense of humour Wayne showed a massive will and determination to complete this race regardless of what was to be put in front of him on some of the brutal days coming up.

★★★

By late afternoon it was time to check our rucksacks again in the highly unlikely event that something had gone missing since the last check carried out a couple of hours ago.

The only other highlights of the afternoon were going for a pee in the desert, buying a MdS Buff at the MdS field shop, fiddling with my Powermonkey solar charger to get it charged up, feeling a couple of slightly less-hot breezes and watching the two MdS camels walk around our part of the bivouac perimeter. We hoped this would be the last time we'd see those camels: if they caught up with you on the course, your race was over.

But then some more excitement arrived! Coupled with the

camel spider incident in the morning this was all a bit too much for one day in the desert.

The kids from a small settlement a couple of miles away had congregated around our side of the bivouac perimeter, keeping a distance away as they'd clearly been warned not to come any closer. Understandably, the rare circus of the MdS train coming to town was an excitement for these poor kids, for whom I imagined not much else went on.

Suddenly we noticed a hubub of activity as the Moroccan police tore across the desert at speed in Land Rovers pursuing some of the kids who were running back towards the settlement. We turned full circle away from our front-of-tent view and settled back onto our sleeping bags and rucksacks to watch the back-of-tent show.

Eventually the police caught up with one young lad holding a bag and unceremoniously bundled him into the Land Rover and drove back towards a tent just a few up from ours. While all this was going on that tent's occupants had been searching the tent for missing items: it seems the kid had got too close, got spooked and run off. He was brought back to the tent but on checking his bag and asking those competitors it was soon resolved he hadn't actually stolen anything. Still, Moroccan police justice was quickly dispensed, just in case, with a couple of cuffs around the head and a couple of kicks up the backside before the kid was allowed to flee.

Show over, we turned back around to the front-of-tent view to see if there were any camel spiders approaching.

* * *

Before long the hours had passed and we were instructed to go to the centre of the bivouac to hear a 5 pm introduction by the MdS's inventor, Race Director Patrick Bauer. Reluctantly, lethargically, we sloped across, water bottles in hand. The organisers started as they meant to go on for the rest of the week: late.

The French announcements were followed by an English translation of a few rules we needed to be aware of (drink plenty: it's going to be very, very hot!) and a few highlights for this year's event: we were told of the oldest competitor amongst us of an incredible 80 years of age who looked a good 20 years younger, and another competitor who was looking to complete his 25th MdS.

There was a considerate, expectant atmosphere all round but standing out in the sun even at this time of day wasn't doing much good for our permanent thumping headaches. The distress flare demonstration passed without incident: there was an audible groan of disappointment as the flare took off safely, competitors instead preferring a repeat of a previous year's demonstration in which the flare went off in its holder, much to the alarm of those giving the demonstration.

The introduction for the 27th MdS over we were now just a few hours away before toeing the start line. Back to the tent we went to prepare, for the umpteenth time, perfectly fine rucksacks in the dying light. There were no breezes at all; almost 6 pm and Mark registered 32.5C in our tent in the shade. It was going to be a warm night.

Our last meal supplied by the organisers at the canteen passed uneventfully; we would now be entirely self-sufficient for our food until a lunch packet was given to us when we finished the final day.

Assuming we finished... We were all very much aware that anything could happen over the next seven days despite the months and years of training committed thus far.

Tired, expectant, excited, we were all in bed by 8 pm.

5

Stage 1: Ammouguer to Oued el Attchana: 33.8 km/21.1m

> *I feel like a child who has found a wonderful trail in the woods. Countless others have gone before and blazed the trail, but to the child it's as new and fresh as if it had never been walked before. The child is invariably anxious for others to join in the great adventure. It's something that can only be understood by actual experience. Those who've begun the journey, and certainly those who've gone further than I, will readily understand what I am saying.*
>
> Randy Alcorn, Money, Possessions and Eternity

Sunday 8 April 2012

Unsurprisingly I had a poor night's sleep. I was awake most of the time. I finally became quite sanguine about it, figuring I'd be so shattered by the end of the day's effort that a good night's sleep was guaranteed.

In that half world of consciousness and sleep I was sure I heard a screeching cockerel crow… in my dream?… was I on holiday in France?

In the confused tangle that was my mind taking an age to deconstruct and reconstruct what was going on I knew something wasn't right: this screeching cockerel couldn't have been taking any breaths; it was a continuous screech of cockadoodle doocockadoodledoo.

A cockerel seemingly performing on a potent cocktail of EPO and steroids, I became more confused as I recognised it was getting louder, much louder.

A weary mutter emerged from a black sleeping bag over to my right, apparently without a head, buried as it was in whatever warmth the sleeping bag was giving. It was Rich.

"What… the… hell… is that?!"

And snap, we were awake.

Three and a half hours to go. Today was the beginning.

It wasn't funny being woken up at 5.30 am, but the grinning maniacal bearded Frenchman driving a Land Rover around the bivouac perimeter, getting closer to us now, clearly felt this was the height of hilarity. His left arm stretched out to a box on his dashboard repeatedly pressing a button which emitted the continuous screech from the large speaker mounted on the roof.

We got used to it after the first few mornings, or maybe we were in too much of a state to notice it.

Time seemed to whip past this morning; before too long we were on the start line with 30 seconds to go.

I dozed for a while as a cold morning warmed up and natural light increased. Before long I figured I'd better crack on with breakfast as once the Berbers arrived the tent would be deconstructed around us, whether we were in it or not.

Two and a half hours to go.

My breakfast preparation, honed after a few attempts at home, was simple enough:

- apply a dollop of alcohol gel to my titanium spork;
- add water to my powdered milk and cereal combination;
- eat;
- bin the empty Poly-Lina breakfast bag;
- clean my spork thoroughly with my tongue then pour a little water onto it for a finger clean;
- apply another dollop of alcohol gel;

- allow to air dry;
- pack.

Quick, simple, stress-free. I'd figured a long time ago that time would be short once I woke up (I'm not the fastest to get up and out of the house, much to my wife's continual amazement) and I really wasn't interested in spending the time trying to boil up a pot of water for breakfast. Some of my tent mates took varying amounts of time with varying degrees of success to boil up their water, depending on the wind direction. Paul, however, took the grand prize for the week in consistently being able to produce a boiling pot of water twice a day in next to no time at all.

Two hours to go.

Once I heard the Berbers starting their approach, a politely audible *Y'allah! Y'allah!* (Let's go! Let's go!) signifying their taking down a tent not too far away, I figured I'd better get my sleeping bag packed away sharpish. Comforting warmth was replaced by a crisp chill air, though this wasn't to be for long. The blankets on the ground would be left in place for a while yet but it wouldn't be fun having the black cotton canvas collapsed around my ears if I didn't move away quick enough.

Now I was up it was a good time to join the fast-moving queue in the centre of the bivouac to collect my first water ration for the day: two 1.5 litre bottles. This had to be done by 7.30 am each morning on pain of a time penalty for failing to comply.

Back at the tent it was time to get changed and ready to race. Again, my routine was intended to be quick and easy but, this being our third day in the desert and with a short while yet before we needed to make our way to the start line, there was no need to crank up our relaxed state.

My night-time looser pair of shorts for sleeping in were exchanged for my tighter Nike running shorts; my T-shirt was exchanged for my long-sleeve shirt; NipGuards were applied; Leukotape was applied to sensitive parts of my feet to reduce the risk of likely areas of blistering; I put on two pairs of socks (my

Thorlos mini-crews over the top of my Injinji "toe socks", comfortably fitting my foot and its toes as a glove does for the hand and its fingers) followed by my one-size larger trainers; sunscreen was applied on any remaining visible skin; I adjusted my sand gaiters; I repacked and adjusted my rucksack, putting my day's running food into my side pockets for quick access and attaching my Powermonkey solar charger to the back.

Done. How refreshingly quick and easy!

One hour to go.

A slightly earlier time for being at the start line was needed to funnel 853 official starters into a carefully laid out pattern of ropes strung across metal poles to form the number "27", signifying this year's 27th Marathon des Sables for the aerial photo.

As we stood there waiting for the aerial photo to be taken I felt suddenly a little queazy, from nerves I think. *This is finally it…* I said to myself. It was something I'd not experienced since standing on the jetty of Gailey Reservoir on a cold Midlands morning at 6 am back in 1999, ready to start The Longest Day Triathlon, my first Ironman-distance event. It was never in my wildest contemplation back then that, 13 years later, I'd be standing on the start line of what was referred to as the toughest footrace on Earth feeling the same thing…

Twenty minutes to go.

After the "27" photo I felt better and we then packed in to the starting pen as variously awful Euro-pop songs began to be played over the loudspeakers. Tent 78 took turns taking various photos.

Fifteen minutes to go.

Patrick Bauer and his English interpreter Alison welcomed us all and said a few words: there were 853 confirmed competitors amongst us from a record 48 countries. Warnings to drink plenty were given. A few birthday announcements followed and 853 people sang "Happy birthday!" to traditional musical accompaniment.

Three minutes to go.

I looked behind me. A few metres away a competitor's colleagues realised too late as their tent mate keeled over backwards, straight as a pole, passed out. It was already in the 30Cs and we were all sweating simply stood there. He's unceremoniously dragged aside across the sand to the Doc Trotters medics. I've no idea if the poor guy started. I pointed this out to my tent mates. Wayne calmly noted his watch was telling him it was now 32C. It wasn't yet 9 am.

Two minutes to go.

Hundreds of competitors were comfortably packed together, ready, primed, rearing to go. The palpable, throbbing excitement and energy was immense, sharp; laughs, screams, cheers variously rang out from this multi-coloured sea of fresh, new racing kit. The unmistakeable gutteral throb of the approaching media helicopter, hovering and swerving around us for aerial shots of the pulsating mass below elicited the required response: various shouts and exclamations, thumbs-up signs on outstretched arms.

"Best of luck guys!" shouted Mark over the noise of the helicopter as we all back-slapped and shook hands.

The 10 second countdown began as AC/DC's *Highway to Hell* boomed around us...

... and we were finally off!

The media helicopter roared away from us. A few hundred metres ahead, for that was where the leading runners already were, the helicopter turned to its side and hovered sideways back toward us, the cameraman perched perilously on the door. More shouts, screams, waves and thumbs-up. The helicopter did this a few times, every morning, and never ceased to elicit the same joyous, excited response.

Once the helicopter had got its opening shots it moved off to be replaced by a relative silence compared with the tumult of the previous half hour: all one could hear now was the sound of hundreds of pairs of running shoes shuffling softly in the sand; the tap-tap-tap-tap of competitors' walking poles across the stony ground; the bubbling excitement of a multitude of foreign tongues.

A tightened pack of 853 competitors gradually strung out across the sand. Focussed determination settled upon us as each competitor came around from the noisy exuberance and remembered running or walking paces and plans. After just a mile few would have noticed the random low-level stone building that had seemingly been deposited in the middle of nowhere to serve no-one, but which was in fact a school which had been equipped from money raised by the 21st Marathon des Sables in 2006, an event in which a mere 25 countries were represented.

I began to warm up with my goal marching pace of four miles per hour alongside Mark and Wayne. Ashley, Paul and Tony, the speedsters of our tent, had already shot off into the distance. Rich and Dean, pictures of strength, had also disappeared speedily into the waves of Raidlight and OMM rucksacks, various designs of sand gaiters and French Foreign Legionnaire-style sunhats.

The scenery was indescribably amazing, nothing like anything I'd yet seen on Earth, a continuation of the sense of uninterrupted space I'd begun to notice on the coach journey out here. It was a marvel to simply look at miles of sand surrounding us, giving way eventually either to more miles of flatness beyond the horizon or low-lying hills, capped by the lightest blue of skies. The natural colours of our surroundings intensified as the sun continued to rise.

Already I seemed to be passing dozens of people and wondered if I should be taking it easier. But I felt supremely fit and strong: *push on, within reason*, I told myself. On occasion the helicopter would sweep by, adding to the sense of amazement and excitement.

Barely half a mile from the start I thought I felt a hot spot and followed the golden rule: I immediately stopped, sat down, carefully took off my shoe and socks, properly inspected the area and found nothing. Better to be safe than sorry later in Doc

Trotter's medical tent. I pulled my socks and shoe back on, slightly tighter to reduce any movement that there had been, and continued on my way.

About four miles from the start an oasis appeared and we followed a narrow path around the abandoned impressive ruins of Ahandar, the fraction of time allowed by its miserly shade very welcome: it was already so hot but barely mid-morning.

We would see several of these small village buildings, abandoned but standing strong, proud and defiant after apparently decades of disuse. Despite being abandoned these tiny deserted villages always seemed to be populated by up to a dozen or so children. I always wondered where they came from: had they travelled especially in the knowledge that the annual big race of the desert was passing through? Or did they always travel far from wherever home was to play in the deserted buildings? This was to become a permanent feature of the race's surroundings: if we were in the middle of nowhere (which the map clearly showed) sometimes a handful of children would appear. How on Earth did they get here? And where from? It was a mystery that was never solved.

Another example of this occurred somewhere after the start and before Checkpoint 2. Just ahead of me I saw a lone young girl stood by the side of the route. Her long, dark unkempt hair shrouded her dark face; she looked tiny with very slim limbs, wearing a simple dress and sandals, and couldn't have been more than 10 years old or so. I wondered where school was and why she wasn't in it, and where her family were. Again, I couldn't understand where she had appeared from and wondered how long she must have been standing there waiting for the MdS circus to pass through; the nearest village according to the map was at least a few miles away. Despite the environment she seemed perfectly happy enough, absent the burden of any Western accoutrements such as a mobile phone constantly held in the hand of a crooked arm in case something happens, jewellery, make-up or handbag.

She was simply standing there with her hands behind her back giving off a huge beautiful smile with gleaming white teeth and big, brown shining eyes, joyous at the unusual sight of a passing throng of mad men and women.

A Canadian chap held in his hand a large clear plastic bag containing what looked like small gold-coloured pieces spotted with red. As he approached the girl he dug out a couple of these small gold-coloured pieces and, her beaming smile and big, brown shining eyes becoming impossibly brighter, she tentatively held out her hands as he dropped these tokens into her palms. She was clearly extremely grateful.

"Canada! From Canada!" the Canadian chap said.

She nodded vigorously and grinned away.

"I'm from Canada. These are from Canada. *From Canada!*" the Canadian chap repeated, with emphasis, at pains to get the message across.

Gleefully, now having understood, she finally responded joyously: "Canada!! Canada!!"

As he trudged on she then almost skipped across the sand with giddy excitement towards me. In her hands I could see that what the Canadian was handing out were pin badges of a red Canadian maple leaf with a gold-coloured backing.

"Hello!" I said.

"Canada! Canada!" she replied, still impossibly grinning and shining away.

"Hi! Hello! How are you?"

"Canada! Canada!" she repeated.

I think the chap's attempt at establishing Canadian/Moroccan diplomatic relations had inadvertently conveyed the idea that "Canada!" was a form of greeting. As I marched onwards the girl bounded on to the competitor behind me greeting him loudly with "Canada! Canada!"

A simple, funny moment.

★ ★ ★

Checkpoint 1 seemed to arrive quickly despite it being almost nine miles from the start. Following my plan once the checkpoint came into view I downed what water I had remaining in my water bottles (meaning I'd consumed 1.4 litres in the first nine miles), able then to pick up my next water ration and dispense it quickly into my bottles (using 1.4 litres, drinking the last 100 millilitres straight away), added my electrolyte tablets and swiftly moved on through.

This ration of 1.5 litres was to see me through to Checkpoint 2, just under seven miles away. I particularly noticed something I hadn't during the previous two days in the bivouac: there were now swarms of buzzing flies everywhere, particularly in the shaded areas of the tents, enjoying the sweat and the stink of a hot mass of humanity. Of course, feeling in pretty good shape by Checkpoint 1 on the first day of our race across the Sahara, pretty much to a man we all dutifully and customarily swatted them away. But it wasn't long before this nod to trying to maintain hygiene was given up.

Shortly after leaving Checkpoint 1 was a gentle ascent across a rocky plateau before it gently descended again. I was coming towards the end of an eight minute fast march and began a run, feeling great. I intended to run two minutes before continuing another eight minute fast march.

I felt fantastic: a warm breeze was ruffling my hat, its protective flaps billowing in the breeze; I could hear my British flag cracking and flapping behind me. Still so early in the race my clothing was in clean, pristine condition. The media helicopter approached from behind and seemed to hover: I looked up to see it start circling me, media cameraman hanging by the door taking some footage. I wondered who it was directed at until I realised it must be me with the next competitors a good 200 metres ahead and behind me. The trouble was by now I was coming to the end of my two minute allotted run. In full view of a worldwide audience do I stop to fast march? Of course I couldn't. I carried on running. *When is this damn helicopter going to move off somewhere else? I want to walk!* The helicopter seemed to hang around for ages as it circled and circled again before moving off. After what seemed five minutes of running I was overheating.

I marched on, by now thoroughly warmed up. The escalating temperature was noticeable yet I was not visibly sweating despite working hard in the unforgiving sun. I needed to remind myself that, with the heat as it is in the desert, sweat simply evaporates almost instantaneously from the skin. Feeling damp and having wet clothes would be no marker of effort or water loss. I later learnt back in the bivouac that the temperature had been recorded as having reached 46C today, said to be the hottest Stage 1 temperature.

I continued with my strategy, running between one and two minutes per block of 10 minutes, the rest a fast march. Our first *jebel* appeared, the *Jebel Bou Lalhirh*. It ascended for just 200 metres with a 15% gradient according to the roadbook: this wouldn't be the first time I wondered if such roadbook statistics were works of fiction conjured for the amusement of the support crew. This was hard work.

The top of this small *jebel* crested to a relatively flat geological fault of dark volcanic rock. The slightly undulating route took us across the edge of this rocky plain but care had to be taken not to be too ambitious with the running: it was a long way down off the side. It was the first time I started to notice significant temperature changes across small changes in elevation: across the top of this *jebel* we were exposed to the warm breeze which was uninterrupted for miles around, but as the route descended barely 10 metres or so into the bowl of the plain the temperature would shoot up. A carefully jogged descent into the bowl became again a fast march or walk as we picked our way across the boulders and stones.

The route finally opened out to the edge of the *jebel*: below us and some three to four miles away we could see Checkpoint 2 shimmering. A technical descent of some 200 metres down the rocky edge saw the temperature climb exponentially: it was remarkable, nothing like anything I'd experienced. A couple of minutes away from having stood on the edge of the *jebel* enjoying a pleasant warm breeze I was now stood at the bottom on the sandy plain: I was baking. I couldn't believe the temperature difference in such a short distance. I could sense the temperature shooting up by degrees as I descended, resembling as it did the opening of an oven door.

I was starting to suffer, barely a few hours from the start. My head started to pound. Was I really dehydrated already? My mouth felt a touch dry, a sure and belated sign that indeed my body was consuming fluid far quicker than I could replace it with my ration. Looking at my water bottles I could see I had about 200 millilitres remaining to see me over the next three miles or so. I took the precaution of abandoning the running efforts and reverted to a fast march across the stony valley to Checkpoint 2.

A line of competitors opened out before me, in varying degrees of competence of walking or shuffling. Already, several were displaying an inability to walk or shuffle in a straight line. For any onlookers such as myself, this was a clear signal that some had underestimated the challenge: *respect the heat and respect the distance; respect the first day, you still have over 140 miles to cover*. Some had clearly misjudged.

I neared a French competitor who looked in bad shape. As I'd approached I'd already seen him projectile vomiting a couple of times at the side of the track.

"*Ca va?*" ("How's it going?") I asked.

As I marched past him I slowed to a walk. He looked gaunt, eyes bloodshot red, comforting his stomach with the palm of his right hand. With a degree of calmness he simply nodded his head in response as I watched his cheeks slowly fill to capacity before he quickly turned and exploded in another fit of projectile vomiting. An impressive display though this looked I did feel sorry for him: to be in this bad a shape so early in the race wasn't a good sign for the odds of completing it.

I marched on, mindful of my own feelings of nausea. Further along I saw a Doc Trotter Land Rover parked up alongside the route. In its sliver of shade I saw another competitor looking wrecked and immensely disappointed, his head hanging loosely down towards his chest, as he sat in a chair being attended to by the Doc Trotter's medics. While the vomiting French competitor I'd seen appeared by his kit and frame to be, like me, a mid- to back-of-the-pack racer, this seated competitor looked very light and lean, both in stature and in rucksack size, in other words a front runner. Separated by just a few minutes I'd seen that the race environment treated all equally harshly, race contender or otherwise.

Barely two or three hours had passed since we crossed the start line of the first stage.

Cresting a small sandy hill I saw Checkpoint 2 a few hundred metres ahead. Finishing off my water I resumed a run to arrive and collect another 1.5 litre water ration. I scanned ahead into the distance: veering off to the right was more flat, sandy plain, but the snake of competitors wasn't going in that direction.

I steeled myself for the challenge ahead: the snake was, unfortunately, slithering in a stop-start fashion, taking a left turn up the side of what appeared to be a steep monster of a mountain, the *Tibert Jebel*, before disappearing. In my experience back home of training up and down Yorkshire moors, that usually meant only one thing: the point at which the snake disappeared was not the end of the ascent.

This time I would need to ration my water carefully: the heat was oppressive and although there were now just (just!) over five miles between me and the finish line of Stage 1 competitors looked in the distance to be suffering up the side of the *Tibert Jebel*.

I took it easy as I approached and took on board a few sweets with my water to fuel up. I intended to pace myself and just keep plodding one foot in front of the other, stopping each time my heart rate hit 160 beats per minute.

It didn't take long for that to happen. Ordinarily, thinking of walking up mountains conjures up images of rocks and stones against which to push off with strong legs to ascend quickly.

I'd never contemplated that a sandy mountain could exist.

True enough, rock was evident along the ascending vertical side of the mountain but the route itself taken to ascend it consisted of just the odd rock dropped in one long, long steeply inclined sandpit. Tracking up the side of this *jebel* there was nowhere to hide: the unrelenting sun, at its strongest of the day, burned away and baked the rock, the sand and those foolish enough to be climbing it. The conversation amongst competitors at the foot of the *jebel* quickly stopped to be replaced by hard breathing, hacking coughs and the odd expletive.

This became incredibly hard work and I laboriously placed one step in front of the other to try and ascend and get this *jebel* over with as quickly as possible. The rucksack on my back, albeit weighing a modest 10 kg or so including my water, wasn't helping at all.

Some simply slumped onto their backs, gasping for breath, mindful of the steep rocky drop off the side; others just sat down, shoulders and head slumped: *I've had enough*. Those who fell onto their hands and knees quickly corrected their resting position as the scorching sand burnt bare skin.

Sure enough the point on the steep track at which the snake of people had disappeared when seen from Checkpoint 2 down below simply showed the point when the track ground onwards and upwards. From the foot of the *jebel* to its summit the track was a mere 0.8 miles but any energy left was being absorbed by this kick in the tail, just a few miles from the finish. There was a palpable feeling all around as we were nearing the end of Stage 1: *what the hell have we let ourselves in for?*

The ascent finally reached, the bivouac and the end of today's Stage 1 came into view: 2.5 miles away from the bottom of the descent across a large open stony plain. This was to be the longest 40 minutes I'd yet experienced.

I wanted to crack on. The descent started off as a rocky very narrow path. Just in front of me a woman with walking poles, completely exhausted, stopped and blocked the route down. Tired, slightly annoyed and without energy enough to be able to utter a polite word I recklessly meandered a little around the rocks to get around her. Others behind me were less accommodating.

Across the stony plain all I could do was walk, ever gradually slower. The finish gantry never seemed to come close enough in proportion to the effort expended to get there. A couple of competitors up ahead started a jog. My competitive spirit got the better of me and so I jogged too, pointlessly trying to preserve whatever place in the rankings I had thus far achieved. I felt very sick from this increase in effort. So, too, did the other competitors who had tried to resume a run. Before long we were just one sporadically spaced line of exhausted walking, stumbling competitors. I couldn't decide which was worse: baking in the heat reflecting off the side of the *jebel* or baking from the heat reflecting up from the lower reaches of the stony plain.

Roasted, I finally passed the finish line with a very sore neck and shoulders, the penalty of slumping up the side of the *jebel* with a rucksack, at a guess. Why didn't I pursue those push-ups and upper body work more vigorously in my training? And would it have made any difference anyway?

I collected my water ration of 4.5 litres and ambled to Tent 78 to crash. Once some semblance of energy returned, which was quicker than I thought, I gradually got myself sorted out: I made up my post-stage *For Goodness Shakes* vanilla carbohydrate and protein drink, consumed more water, changed into my looser shorts and warmer T-shirt and aimed to keep my legs slightly raised as much as I could by propping them on the tent poles or my rucksack to try and reduce inflammation and soreness.

Mark had heard a rumour that there was an old desert well a couple of hundred metres away, which despite our tired legs sounded too good to be true. So myself and Mark wandered towards the alleged site and, excitedly, we spotted a strongly-built square of old stone where other competitors were hoisting up a couple of decades-worn leather buckets from the watery depths.

Like men and women returning ashore from months at sea, we gazed in awe at others dousing themselves in what was obviously freezing cold cleansing water. When it was finally our turn Mark and I firstly washed our stinking filthy kit (as it was after just one day in the sands) and then poured a bucket of the freezing cold water over each other: it was absolutely chilling and hence, in what felt now a far cooler but pleasantly warm late afternoon, revitalising. We did this a couple of times, aware that this was probably the last desert well we would come across for the rest of the week.

Having by now had a bit of food and taken on more water, I felt a world away from the miserableness of trudging the last 2.5 miles from the bottom of the *jebel*. Mark and I both agreed that Stage 1 seemed to be a particularly tough one. Back at our tent our washed kit was dry in no time hanging out on the tent ropes.

* * *

Strong late afternoon winds roared up in no time at all (we were, after all, sat in the middle of a huge desert plain) so it was all hands on deck to sort out the annoyance: without a collection of stones and rocks to weigh them down the black cotton sides of our tent flapped up and let in half the desert. We were still at the stage where, psychologically, getting sand on everything really did seem to matter.

With all of us now back at the tent after the day's effort Tony had some stunning news. Tony, the Marathon des Sables veteran from 2011, had decided to quit. This was a bit of a shock. When asked why by all of us, concerned, he simply said:

"I know what's coming. I did it last year and I just don't feel motivated to do it again."

I think this shook us all a little. Here was a guy who was clearly very fit, one of the faster in the field, and completed this race last year. If he was quitting because he knew what was coming… we all gulped at that, particularly with how hard Stage 1 had just been. We all tried to convince him to stay and continue, if only because of the money spent to enter the race in the first place (£3,500 for 2012).

Sadly, Tony couldn't be convinced to stay. More gulps from the rest of us followed. Fortunately Tony was able to stay on a few more days because of the practical point that it would be incredibly difficult to drive a beaten up old Mercedes masquerading as a taxi to pick him up in the middle of the desert. He would have to wait until the course meandered a little closer to a "road" (or, as we would know it, a dirt track).

Before long dusk was coming. I wrote up my diary for the day and boiled up a pot of water to enjoy my rehydrated freeze-dried spaghetti bolognese meal followed by a coconut energy bar. As we all enjoyed our meals Wayne had a funny story to tell.

He had been plodding up the *Tibert Jebel* feeling sorry for himself when he came to stop for a rest. A French Foreign Legionnaire-type bellowed at him from a Land Rover:

"*Why are yoo he-air? Becos yoo thot thees wood be eezzee? Nor! Yoo air he-air becos eet eez HARD! Eef eet waz eezzee, then efferee wun wood do eet!!!*"

Suitably chastised, Wayne powered on to finish in fear of being thrown off the side of the *jebel*.

The usual tent chat resumed until it was lights out, all of us exhausted, around 8pm.

What had we let ourselves in for?

★ ★ ★

GARMIN FORERUNNER 310XT STATISTICS FOR STAGE 1

Distance: 21.14 miles
Time: 6 hours, 3 minutes, 1 second
Elevation gain: 1323 feet
Calories burnt: 4166
Heart Rate Average: 147 beats per minute
Heart Rate Maximum: 171 beats per minute

OFFICIAL RACE STATISTICS

Stage 1 finish position: 496 of 853 starters
Finish time: 6 hours, 3 minutes, 3 seconds
Stage 1 abandonments: 5

6

Stage 2: Oued el Attchana to Taourirt Mouchanne: 38.5 km/24 miles

Come what may, all bad fortune is to be conquered by endurance.
Virgil

Monday 9 April 2012

It had been a very warm night, which meant not sleeping very well in the constant fight for a constant body temperature. I found myself moving from too hot at around midnight to too cold in the freezing desert air at around 4 am. Again. I also kept getting up to go and urinate, a lot, which didn't help in the quest for sleep. But at least I was rehydrating properly.

The electronic cockerel and the grinning Land Rover-wielding Frenchman woke us all up too early. Again. The Berbers dismantled the tent while some of us were still in it. Groggily, we all eventually came around to face a 24 mile run across the desert. I think all of us in Tent 78 felt largely fine though, recuperated enough from not having to do anything else yesterday other than lie down and take it easy after a Stage 1 hard effort.

We made our way to the start line for the appointed time and various announcements. It was said that yesterday's Stage 1 saw the highest number of abandonments of competitors for a Stage 1 in the history of the Marathon des Sables. It seems hard to believe when there were only five abandonments, but it says something about what is the usual degree of difficulty of Stage 1: historically most abandons had occurred later in the race.

We were warned that today would be hot with an unusually high humidity. I'm not sure we assembled competitors had any real inkling of what that meant. We figured that considering it's hot in the desert anyway, a pre-race warning that it was to be hot meant it was going to be, well, *very hot*. In fact, such was the race organiser's concern about what would be today's heat the start time was brought forward by 30 minutes. That wasn't to prove to be as helpful to many competitors perhaps as the organisers might have liked, including me.

The birthday announcements gave way to a chorus of "Happy Birthday!" from the remaining 848 starters. AC/DC's *Highway to Hell* signified the 30 second countdown to start and the unrestrained enthusiasm and excitement was then unleashed upon the desert sands.

The roadbook suggested a relatively flat Stage 2 overall with two separate areas of small sand dunes. I felt in good form following yesterday's effort. With a largely flat stage I felt I could increase the running element for today while keeping enough effort in the tank for the rest of a long week.

It wasn't long after the start though that what the roadbook described as "sandy with camel grass" resembled more a sand bog with lacerating strips of camel grass sitting atop uneven humps: it was nigh on impossible to keep any running momentum going or a direct line across this part of the course. But I was quickly building on my experience from yesterday's Stage 1 of which types of sand would take my weight long enough to remain firm and allow some fast marching: the darker crust of untrodden sands seemed to hold well, where they existed. Everything else was just a slog.

Checkpoint 1 soon appeared and still feeling quite fresh I

didn't stay long, just enough time to refill my water bottles and get some sugars into me. I felt perfectly fine; hot, but otherwise fine.

It was clear before I'd even started that the section described in the roadbook as "small dunes" between Checkpoints 1 and 2 was going to be even harder work. The distance between the two checkpoints at just 4.3 miles gave the game away when there was a standard issue 1.5 litres of water at Checkpoint 1. Ordinarily the distance between checkpoints in this year's event and thus water ration issue was around 6.25-7.5 miles. It doesn't sound much when committed to paper, but the expectation that 1.5 litres of water would be needed for just 4.3 miles when it would normally cover around 6.25-7.5 miles was a warning, with big red flashing lights and sirens.

These dunes were tough, grinding, repetitive and rolled on seemingly endlessly. I'd given up trying to run as the constant undulation of sand dunes interrupted my rhythm. I had no idea that covering 4.3 miles across rough terrain could take so long. My gaiters were doing a fantastic job of keeping the sand out but the constant up-down-up-down-up-down of ascending and descending sand dunes which didn't exceed much more than ten to twenty feet in height was sapping a lot of my energy. There didn't seem to be much in the way of a direct dune-free line; any that existed I took but it still meant ploughing through deep, soft sand.

Around me people were struggling. As seemed to happen yesterday while crossing the volcanic rock, the temperature felt to be climbing ever upwards in a very short space of time, as if someone had whacked up the setting on the huge oven that we were running in: again, there was a noticeable difference between the temperature standing atop a dune and the temperature at its base although there was barely ten to twenty feet in distance between the two.

I was wary of drinking too much water too soon, concerned at how long it was taking me to get through this dune field in temperatures which at midday hit an officially recorded 38.7C. I didn't know this at that time, and neither did I know that it was to get a lot hotter still before the day was out.

In the last mile or so of these rolling dunes my rejuvenated self of just a few hours ago at the start line was getting a little despondent: my legs were working hard, I couldn't run, I started to get quite concerned at how little water I had left. It was so damn hot and stifling, clawing at every inch of my body and rising mercilessly from the ground. My lungs were taking gulps of hot dry air that removed what little moisture I had left in my mouth and throat; my hands had visibly swelled; my trainers, one size larger than normal, now had no room in them at all for any further swelling of my feet. There was absolutely no shade to be had. My head pounded painfully. I knew from my GPS watch that Checkpoint 2 couldn't be far now but my mind was concerned at my lack of water: I became concerned at how bad I felt. I desperately wanted more water, but couldn't yet have it.

Atop another "small" dune I just caught sight of the tops of the flags of Checkpoint 2. There were just three or four of these damn sand dunes to clear and I'd be there. I felt a little relieved. I overtook a couple of competitors in the shuffle towards Checkpoint 2 and my tracking chip bleeped as I crossed the line.

I collected my 1.5 litre water ration, having barely wetted my mouth from what was left in my bottles as I approached Checkpoint 2. I wanted more. This ration simply didn't feel enough and I began to recognise that I was a long way down the road to dehydration. I shuffled along to the oppressive heated shade of a tent and flopped carelessly down, barely finding room enough to sit: it was busy here. There must have been 10 or so competitors sat in that tent, variously addressing wounds, blisters, water bottles. Some held their heads in their hands. One or two were in tears. Others stared out to nothing in particular. Other than the odd expletive muttered every now and then, no one was talking. We had firmly entered the hells of MdS legend: not enough food, not enough water, not enough sleep, too much heat.

I looked across to the other tent in the hope of seeing a bit more room for me to sort out my water bottles but this tent was for Doc Trotter's visitors only. It was full of competitors, variously grimacing and crying out as the medics attended them. Others were or had been in tears. A couple of competitors behind me moved on and I leant back, propped on my rucksack and refilled my water bottles, emptying the little that was left over my head. The cooling relief of pouring very warm, sun-heated water over my far hotter head was immediate, but the relief passed very quickly as the water dried in no time. A competitor sat behind me leant back too and accidentally snapped the British flag poking out of my rucksack; I felt somehow detached from myself as a part of me felt I should have been ever so slightly annoyed (though it was simply an accident) but my consciousness refused to summon any annoyance or even acknowledgement that my prized flag had snapped. Maybe a few days in the desert was already changing my perspective of what mattered, or of what I could realistically change after something had happened.

By now we had all given up any attempt at swatting away the swarms of flies that were all around us, buzzing angrily and noisily around us, settling on our bodies, our water bottles or partially wrapped food. I was really past caring about what were now trifling annoyances such as swarms of flies.

Having rested too long I hauled myself up, put on my sun hat and glasses and consulted my roadbook: in a straight line immediately ahead of me was Checkpoint 3, six miles away. It dawned on me that I couldn't actually see the other side of this dried-up lake (the *Ma'der El Kebir* lake) and hence I couldn't see Checkpoint 3: the winds were whipping up a sand storm in the distant mirage and the cloud of sand was getting closer all the time.

I trudged on to follow the distant competitors in a straight line.

As the sand storm approached and my legs and face began to sting from the flying particles of sand I adjusted my Buff tightly around my face, glasses and hat and trudged on. Sand blasted into the little exposed skin I had with every whip of wind, my hands and legs now taking the brunt. Visibility dropped.

There are no words that can describe the heat I experienced crossing this dried lake. The image of Ralph Fiennes stumbling across the desert muttering "Catherine!" in the film *The English Patient* randomly popped into my head.

Any time was too long to be spent out in this flatness of cracked ground. The sandstorm seemed quite short-lived, 10 minutes or so, but my lungs had still taken on sand despite my precautions. As the sand storm settled I could feel the heat mirroring up again from the sandy floor around me, my shoes seemed to be absorbing a lot of it, and the sun combined with this intense ambient heat as the sand storm finally disappeared to create yet another furnace-like experience.

I didn't know it at the time but the temperature recorded hit 52C at that dried lake bed. I was reminded of my attempts to acclimate in the humidity of the Turkish baths back home and was glad to have done so: while I was suffering some salt losses my clothes didn't have too many signs of the tell-tale streaks of white salt loss marks; a few competitors I passed seemed to have leached salt all over their clothes. This 50-odd C of dry heat was very different with a comparatively low humidity; very uncomfortable while at the same time just about bearable. A few competitors around me seemed to be finding it too much as they started to meander all over the place in attempts to walk in a straight line. This would be me before long. Later, tales would circulate the bivouac of competitors collapsing onto the desert floor, attended minutes later by the medics with IV drips.

"March or die" is what I thought at the time. I also started to question, momentarily, why the hell I signed up for this.

During this trek across the dried lake, in the far distance to the east, I spotted a couple of wild camels walking across the plain.

"Wow!" I thought, "Wild camels!" and took a couple of pictures with my disposable camera (none of which developed very well), not knowing that I was soon to pass through a stinking oasis full of them at close proximity.

I don't recall being aware that I was slipping into trouble, other than an acute awareness of oppressive heat and the inability to get fully hydrated which began somewhere between Checkpoint 1 and 2. I couldn't recall the last time I'd urinated despite the amount of water I'd consumed overnight and this morning, perhaps around six litres or more: was it earlier that morning, before the race started?

My conscious thinking was becoming very cloudy. I didn't really feel visually aware of what was around me. My mind seemed to be closing in. Checkpoint 3 must have appeared, my plastic punch card said I arrived there, and I would have collected another water ration: I just don't have any recollection of it at all. In fact I later learnt that an extra bottle of water was dispensed here, so three litres of water, because the conditions were so fierce: I recall nothing about this but, for me, the extra was already too late.

From this point, Checkpoint 3, the wheels really did start to fall off. I picked my way through a rough and dried mud track and oasis with dozens of incredibly stinking camels and donkeys all around me. Some of the camels got a little too close for comfort but fortunately they became spooked before I did. Unfortunately that seemed to create a stampede of running camels and donkeys, which was slightly unsettling as I trudged on through a chaotic mass of thundering hooves. Luckily none of them were blind, not that I had the energy or presence of thought to move much out of their way.

Then I came across the last sand dunes and camel grass section of the day: five miles of the stuff.

In what seemed an alarmingly short space of time I was almost completely out of energy and started to find it a real struggle to put one foot in front of the other over the sand dunes. I didn't want to eat anything. I knew I was dehydrated but I really couldn't face taking more swigs of water and swallowing salt tablets. My water bottles were now giving off a very strong plastic smell and taste as they had cooked to a softer plastic while I crossed the dried lake bed: putting my mouth anywhere near them was making me feel ill. Or was I taking on too much water and salt tablets? Confusion took over as I struggled to recall what Mike Stroud may have written about this in his book *Survival of the Fittest*. Or was it a different book I'd read? Should I force more water down me or ease off it a while? Should I take more salt tablets? Any sugary food? I simply couldn't remember and became increasingly frustrated in my attempts to remember very simple, basic facts.

I found myself stopping several times and waiting for my energy to resume before plodding on. I felt very sick. I sat down for a few minutes on a dune to admire the views. I saw the finishing bivouac but no matter how hard I tried I couldn't get any closer to it. Why was it so far away? And why didn't it get ever closer despite putting one foot in front of the other?

This pattern continued for what seemed like an eternity: walk a bit; stop; walk a bit; stop; sit down; try and drink a few sips; get up; breathe; walk a bit; stop; and so on.

While writing this book and researching a couple of points I came across Eoin Scott's blog of his 2012 Marathon des Sables and immediately recognised whom Eoin was talking about. I distinctly remember sitting down a few times as competitors carried on to pass me, absorbed in their own difficulties to get to the finish line.

But on one particular sitting session I was steeling myself to do so for the last time and simply looked ahead at the distant finish gantry of Stage 2, mentally muttering to myself all sorts of positive thoughts to get me up for the last time and keep one foot placed in front of the other until I got to my tent. I remember feeling very tight in my neck and upper shoulders and during my sit down put my hands behind my head in a futile attempt to stretch off my aches. Two competitors walked past, one of whom I recognised as he was mentioned to me the previous day as a fellow Ironman veteran. With the finish line in view they asked how I was and I replied I was fine, that I was just resting. This is Eoin's view of what he saw:

"About 1km away from the day's finish line we came across a competitor looking absolutely spaced out just resting on a small dune. Not normal behaviour when you're so close to the end. Asking him if he was OK, it was the "Yeah, just resting a few minutes", and at that point he put his hands behind his head and laid down on the dune. Mmmmm not the best of signs. Now dilemma time for me! There was a Doc Trotter sand buggy not far away, do I say something to them or just let the guy lie there and hope he sees sense and gets going again? Lets face it, I hid from them the day before so I didn't want to put someone's race at risk, but I didn't want someone to get ill out there either. I decided to say I was concerned about someone further back in the field but I couldn't see his race number or name, so if he had got going again they wouldn't know it was him, but if he was in difficulty they could help him and hopefully get him to move that final 1.5km and then get medical help in the bivouac."

I was resting a few minutes on each occasion I stopped. Eoin's sighting must have been the last time I stopped as, according to the stage results, he and his companion Peter finished the stage just five minutes ahead of me.

I picked myself up and pushed on, summoning whatever energy I had left to move ever further forward to that finish line. When I think now as I write this, in the cold northern UK climate, it seems incredible that just a single mile seemed so incredibly hard to cover, but incredibly hard it was. I think the resting must have done me some good: I recall that in this last mile or so I felt a little cooler, whether because of a drop in the ambient temperature (it's all relative: a drop from 52C to the high-30Cs feels cool!) or because I'd recovered a little.

I certainly though didn't feel right. I crossed the Stage 2 finish line and Eoin's message to one of the medical team must have worked as I now recall a couple of medics homing in on me immediately after I finished. They asked if I was okay. I said I was and just needed to rest, having found it very hot and that I was feeling sick. They guided me (I don't recall having had a choice) to the side of the Sultan tea van and I was given a hot sweet tea. A couple of sips of something that wasn't plain water tasted good. I shivered suddenly with an odd cold sensation; I really wanted to get back to my tent.

I stood up and hobbled to the truck that was dispensing the 4.5 litres of water ration. I only recall a few things with clarity after this.

I'd walked barely 100 metres over the finish line, now clutching my three water bottles. Suddenly, violently, I dropped the lot and fell to my hands and knees and vomited profusely: a pile of syrupy water shot before me. I looked across to my left as I heard a Berber ask if I was okay.

I vomited again, less profusely. I believe I passed out, collapsing unconscious on the ground momentarily. I don't really know. I do know though that the next thing I was aware of was being hoisted up from the ground by one arm by the Berber and the other arm by a medic (where did she come from?), who must have been closely hovering watching my every move to get there that quick. I was confused, wondering how I had moved from being on my hands and knees retching to being flat on the ground and being hauled up. I was dragged across the sand, the toes of my shoes leaving drag lines, until I was able to take a few steps in time with my handlers with the urgent rush to get me onto a camp bed in the nearby medical tent.

In broken French and English I tried to explain to the two French medics what had happened: they took a look at my water bottles on my rucksack; observing them they looked concerned.

"When did you last drink?" a medic, whom I later knew to be called Lisbeth, asked.

I tried to explain, but my jaw was oddly tight and unable to move or utter much, that I'd last had a good swig of water a couple of hours ago but had only been taking small sips for the last hour. I could think that this was what I wanted to say, but my jaw and mouth couldn't move too well to utter much.

They looked incredulous and alarmed and shook their heads until I could finally explain I had continued to take sips. Miscommunication meant they were horrified at the idea of someone not having drunk anything at all for at least two hours.

I became aware of a piercing on my hand as one medic took some blood samples while the other gently pulled open my mouth and dabbed my tongue with her gloved finger. Some words were exchanged in French too complicated for me to understand before some "tut-tuts" were uttered with more shakes of the head. Apparently the dryness of my mouth and whatever my blood sample was telling them was now giving concern.

I was hauled up again and, by now able to take gentle steps, guided to a waiting Land Rover and driven the barely 100 metres back towards the finish area and sea of medical tents. In I went, guided to a field bed. One of my water ration bottles, a precious 1.5 litres, was taken and filled with a salt solution. I was asked to drink it.

I did, but within seconds I flopped myself off the field bed onto my knees, forcing apart the plastic sheets forming the wall of the medical tent, and vomited yet again onto the sand. This time I brought up the last two salt tablets I'd taken some time ago, sat there on the sand still pristinely white and undigested. I vomited again, by now my stomach in severe cramping pains. The medic who'd brought me in took a look at my produce: we admired it together and as I looked at her I somehow conveyed the message "Look! I *have* been taking my salt tablets!"

The medics seemed to go into overdrive at this point. Something wasn't right. Feeling very weak and lapsing into either unconsciousness or sleep I was hoisted onto a lower-lying field bed as another medic rolled up with a box of intravenous (IV) bags, tore it open and put one up onto the IV pole that had been wheeled up. I wasn't asked if I wanted an IV drip, as James Cracknell was when he ended up in the same situation after Stage 4 during his 2010 Marathon des Sables. I didn't seem to have a choice in this: they were damn well going to give me one whether I liked it or not! So I guess I must have been in a poor state.

I was too out of it to say anything and I knew my day's efforts to get over the finish line in a respectable time, despite the difficulty I was having, would be harmed by an automatic two hour penalty for having taken an IV drip.

I had that feeling again of the world passing in slow motion as a long needle with what looked to me an unusually large hole descended, tautening my skin immediately before it punctured a hole into my right arm. I was told I was going to have five bags of 500ml of IV fluid and they'd see how I was after that. I didn't know it at the time but five bags was your lot: taking more than that would mean disqualification. A little later I learnt of an Israeli competitor, used to training in the harsh temperatures of his homeland, who was administered seven bags of 500ml of IV drip and hence was disqualified. He couldn't understand how he'd got to that physical position considering his hot weather training.

As I laid there taking bag after bag of IV drip what was by now clearly the designated IV drip tent gradually began to fill up. Before long it was a groaning throng of vomiting, semi-conscious competitors being administered with IV drips by their accompanying medics.

It was a bad day for many.

I don't know for certain but I must have been in there for about four to five hours. As the fourth bag began to drip away I became a little concerned: I didn't really feel much better. I started feeling very cold and started shivering. A medic gave me an aluminium sheet to get warm again. Without any awareness of it, I fell into a deep sleep.

Click, whir, click, whir, click, whir, FLASH! click, click, click, whir, FLASH! FLASH!

What the… ?!?!

I was woken by a media photographer standing to my left taking photos of me… close up. As I came around she looked a little sheepish but then professional instincts must have taken over and she carried on clicking anyway. I also caught sight of a second and third media photographer standing at the foot of my bed before I was blinded by another flash of a camera. Standing next to them was a video cameraman taking his footage. A flicker of annoyance may have registered on my face but I was still too shattered to say or do anything. A couple more photos were taken and they moved off to another victim.

At this point the medic Lisbeth returned, my fourth bag having been empty for some time, and my fifth bag was strung up to the IV drip lines. I must have been gradually coming around to some semblance of normality: I knew what I had to do if I wanted to continue in the race.

"Are you feeling better?" Lisbeth asked.

"Oh! yes, much better thank you! I can't believe the difference!"

I feigned a recovery I did not yet feel. I was starting to feel better but definitely didn't feel like getting back to my tent, let alone getting up tomorrow to run almost 22 miles. Impressions, I felt, were what mattered in front of the Doc Trotters medics. But who was I kidding? These professionals would know in the morning, as I was picked out and marked on approaching them to collect my day's water ration, whether they felt I was fit enough to continue ("*Watch that one, competitor number 514…* ").

About half way through the fifth bag I did suddenly brighten up; I wasn't fully with it, but sufficiently with it to know I could get up and get going again. I just felt incredibly tired and a lack of food meant I was ravenous: I hadn't eaten anything substantial for over 12 hours now and my body would have burnt in excess of at least 3000 calories in the meantime.

While I lay there I became aware of pain. Adrenaline had worn off; my body was awakening to the ordeal it was being put through. The nasty deep blister I picked up on the Grantham Ultra the previous month on my right heel and which hadn't healed before I came out here reminded me firmly it was still there.

Lisbeth, who had been looking after me, very kindly agreed to sort it out. While doing so she told me that she'd been volunteering for the Marathon des Sables medical team for several years and she'd never seen so many IV drips having to be dispensed so early in the race: commonly this amount would be usual by the Stage 4 long stage as dehydration and water rationing over several days took its cumulative effect. It had been a tough day out there and the unusually high temperatures so early in the race had affected many more than expected.

At some point Rich and Dean had found me to see if I was okay, which was very thoughtful of them. They'd brought me my email which included a message from my wife which, in my delicate state, made me tearful. They kindly took my rucksack back to the tent: the thought of hobbling back with it for a few hundred metres once I was finished in the medical tent wasn't attractive.

Having had five bags of IV drip I now put on my best smile and a convincing enough performance for the medics to allow me to wander back to my tent. The medical tent remained though fully occupied with IV drips being given to a number of other delirious competitors.

Getting back to Tent 78 took a long while: in sending back my rucksack with Rich and Dean I'd forgotten to take out my headtorch. Stumbling around in the pitch black I gradually made out in the distance the dim outline of some tents and a few fires and so I headed in that direction: Tent 78 would be there somewhere or, if I missed it, the neighbouring country of Algeria. I didn't really care.

Eventually I found my tent and feeling positively awful dumped myself in the remaining space my tent mates had left for me. I felt guilty because I was now going to wake them up by trying to cook up one of my dehydrated meals. I tried to do it a reasonable distance away from the back of our tent to not disturb them, realising before long that I was cooking up in an area where most of this part of the bivouac had likely been relieving themselves for the last few hours. I still couldn't have cared less.

I ate most but not all of a poorly rehydrated meal and tried to get to sleep. I felt wretched. After a couple of hours my body decided to have a spate of violent diarrhoea. The positive I took from it was that I wasn't also vomiting at the same time so that, I felt, was a good sign.

And that was my night: drifting in and out of dozing, falling asleep, waking up and having a bout of diarrhoea in a recurring pattern until well into the early hours of the morning. By that time my regular intake of Immodium melts seemed to have done the trick of blocking me up for very likely a week.

When I finally felt that uninterrupted sleep was coming I assessed where I was. I was incredibly tired, yet frustratingly really couldn't sleep. My painful stomach was doing somersaults: the earlier vomiting cramps had done some damage. My badly blistered heel was painful to walk on, a feeling of shards of glass burying themselves into raw blistered and bloody flesh as I hobbled. I was on a cycle of sweating because I was too hot and shivering because I was too cold. After today's effort I felt completely drained, like I never had before.

Other people had called it a day. Tony, our Marathon des Sables veteran, had quit after the first day knowing what was coming up. Why couldn't I? I'd trained, I'd arrived, I ended up on an IV drip for more than four hours. It's not as if I'd be going home in shame. I could always come back next year. Maybe I'd pushed myself too hard on Stage 1 and now I was suffering for it. What would my family and friends think? I knew they wouldn't be surprised nor think anything less of me: this event was tough stuff to have to contend with. It wasn't referred to as the toughest footrace on Earth for nothing.

As I fell asleep, unconvincingly I thought about quitting but resolved to make a decision in the morning. I was utterly exhausted.

★★★

GARMIN FORERUNNER 310 XT STATISTICS FOR STAGE 2

Not known.

OFFICIAL RACE STATISTICS

Stage 2 finish position: 813 of 848 starters
Finish time: 9 hours, 41 minutes, 18 seconds (including a 2 hour time penalty for having received an IV drip)
Stage 2 abandonments: 15

7

Stage 3: Taourirt Mouchanne to El Maharch: 35 km/21.8 miles

The first virtue in a soldier is endurance of fatigue; courage is only the second virtue.

Napoleon Bonaparte

Tuesday 10 April 2012

I finally woke up having had a good and solid two to three hours of sleep, what must have been the longest uninterrupted period for several nights. I also awoke not feeling at all committed to the idea of quitting: that wasn't in my nature. It didn't take long to mentally prepare myself for this: *quit? Don't be ridiculous…* But I knew I would have to treat my body with greater care, if I were to complete the Marathon des Sables, and simply hope that mental stamina and bloody mindedness would continue to triumph to direct my body to do what I wanted it to do.

My tent mates asked how I felt and I said I was fine but had thought about quitting. Even *thinking*, let alone *uttering* the word "quitting" felt alien and very wrong.

There was a chorus from my tent mates: *you can't give up! Don't do that: you'll regret it!*

Mark was particularly adamant, pointing out all the effort, sacrifice, training and money spent to get this far. Tony was very wise in his views: just get some breakfast eaten, get going, get to the start line, take it easy and see how you feel by Checkpoint 1. This was excellent advice.

This also sounded just what I wanted to hear: I simply wanted others to assist in enforcing my mental resolve. If they'd agreed it might be wise to quit, my contrarian nature would inevitably have reacted: I would have started the day's stage anyway simply to prove a point. I was, after all, still alive. I hadn't died and I wasn't now in a life-threatening situation: the possibility I might have been at some point in the previous 12 hours didn't cross my mind. I'd simply been unwell for a period. The thought of quitting became unthinkable. The organisers would have to drag me off the course.

Once awake I at first still felt incredibly weary and dehydrated but, after a good drink of warm water and some cold breakfast, and considering what I'd been through the previous day, I felt surprisingly good overall. Relatively speaking. I rested as long as I could before I really had to get up and made a conscious effort to sip every drop of water I had left from my previous day's ration.

I wandered over to the centre of the bivouac just before 7.30 am to collect the day's first water ration of 1.5 litres, just in time to avoid a lateness penalty. I still had, from the previous evening, a salty bottle of water: you'll recall that when I got to the medical tent one of my three bottles of end-of-stage water ration had had salts added to it, a few sips of which made me vomit.

I had since drunk just a little of this solution and managed to keep the concoction inside me. I'd also used a little for cooking but it was tough trying to drink any more of what was left: it tasted disgusting. With half a bottle of this remaining I asked the medic at the water checkpoint (not the kindly Lisbeth but the more no-nonsense of the two who'd helped me the previous day) if I could have it replaced: I hadn't, after all, actually asked for one of my three bottles of precious water ration to have salts added. It was just done without any consideration of what I thought or wanted.

She agreed that, yes, it could be replaced if I brought it over to her. Jubilant in thinking I'd get another 1.5 litres to finish off before today's start I quickly returned to my tent and came back with my half empty 1.5 litre contaminated water bottle.

The medic took my bottle and held it up to the sunlight before allowing the water to level. With a pen she then marked a horizontal line where the water now sat. It began to dawn on me that my grand plan wasn't going to work.

She got hold of another unopened bottle of water and, slowly, began to wet the sand as she poured out water from this new bottle. Precious, clean water wasting into the sand... Periodically she would stand the two bottles on the flat surface of the Land Rover's bonnet. Cruelly, the process seemed to take an age. Eventually, the level of the water in my contaminated bottle matched the level in the clean, new bottle. With a smile she handed me the clean, new bottle with exactly the same amount of water that was in the contaminated water I had brought over. She then poured out the remains of the contaminated water into the sand.

Crestfallen, I simply said "Thank you!" and returned to my tent. It was logical, of course: I don't think in the circumstances I should have had any more water than any of my competitors but, all the same, it was hard to watch.

Before long we were shuffling over to the start line. The previous two day's of striding purposefully to the start line had by now become a procession of weary, shuffling legs with 45 miles in them. The pain in my right heel subsided as exercise and adrenaline combined to gradually dull the sensation of stabbing needles in my raw bloody blister.

By now, lining up at the start of Stage 3, we recognised that no day was going to start on time so it was a case of relaxing and going with the flow. Impatience at the lack of a prompt start was a futile waste of energy. However, not passing the odd moan about Gallic approaches to time-keeping was impossible: we all knew that a 20 minute or half an hour delay in starting from the advertised start

The author carrying out his water bottle hygiene routine
(© Richard Cairns)

A long way down from the cool to the long expanse of heat on Stage 3
(© Mark Dymond)

The author: exhausted, somewhere in the Sahara . . .
(© Mark Roe)

A long ascent is followed by a quick, steep, sandy descent on Stage 4
(© Mark Dymond)

Pristinely clean before the start of Stage 1: (from left to right) Wayne, the author, Ash, Tony, Rich (crouching), Paul, Dean and Mark (© Mark Roe)

Stinking and dirty, minus Tony, on the morning of the final stage: (from left to right) Rich, the author, Mark, Paul, Ash, Wayne and Dean (© Ashley Wager)

Finished, with the medal to prove it!
(© Emma Roe)

Peaceful, relaxed, finished, smiling!
(© Emma Roe)

time meant we would be out in the fiercest heat of the day for longer than should have been necessary.

Standing in the escalating heat there were the usual announcements, including birthday celebrations. On a more serious note we were told that 15 competitors had to abandon yesterday, forced by the organisers or otherwise, and so there were 833 starters this morning. We were implored to keep sipping regularly as today was expected to have conditions very similar to those of yesterday.

As the countdown began I reconstructed my race plan, slightly. Today I would take it easy: in the last 12 hours I had vomited a lot, had bouts of diarrhoea, probably been unconscious (albeit briefly) and on an IV drip for several hours. As Mark, Paul and Wayne agreed, it was amazing I was even standing there.

So I promised myself to take it easy: march fast, yes, but no running until at least having got past Checkpoint 1… or maybe in sight of Checkpoint 1… or perhaps when the roadbook map told me Checkpoint 1 was just around the corner…

By now I felt immeasurably better: the difference between how I felt when I finally nodded off in the early hours of this morning and seconds before the starting gun was immense.

This didn't mean though I could start off nudging my limits: I fully intended to take it easier today and, assuming all went well, I thought of gradually increasing my speed as the rest of the week progressed. I wanted to regain those 200 places or so that I'd lost yesterday following the two hour time penalty for having had an IV drip. I should have stuck to the original plan from the beginning of Stage 1 and built gradually into the event. But Stage 1 had felt deceptively straightforward until the last couple of miles and that may have been my undoing on Stage 2… coupled with the temperatures hitting the mid-50Cs across that damn dried lake bed.

A long straight route took us across energy-sapping sandy terrain and vegetation from the off until Checkpoint 1 appeared at

12 km, where I met Mark and Wayne. The couple of medics and volunteers who'd greeted me through the finish line yesterday cheered me through, asked how I was and remarked how much better I looked compared to yesterday.

I looked over at Wayne and it seemed accumulated fatigue was starting to take a toll: he didn't look his usual chipper self. I asked if he was okay and simply got a few nods; Mark said he was going to keep him company for a while.

This relatively straightforward terrain should have felt easy but we were all now suffering from the compounded trials of the previous few days: the inescapable heat that was constantly with us, poor sleep and of pushing ourselves daily over distances most people wouldn't cover once in their lifetimes.

All this was now taking its toll: there wasn't the brash rush from the start as there had been on Stages 1 and 2. Everyone seemed to be taking it a bit easier, perhaps bearing in mind that plenty would need to remain in the tank for tomorrow's dreaded 51 mile Stage 4.

We were given two bottles of 1.5 litres of water at Checkpoint 1: a sign of difficulties ahead as Checkpoint 2 was 8.5 miles away.

The line of competitors veered left from Checkpoint 1 in a north/north-easterly direction, ascending up a deceptively steep sandy then stony then rocky route to the panoramic summit view of *Jebel Zireg*. I was feeling quietly confident and, odd as it felt, I was beginning to feel markedly stronger by each step. I was diligently sipping away at my water, eating regularly and continuing to take the salt tablets and my electrolytes. I with a few others took a slightly deviating but more direct but boulder-strewn route to the bottleneck of a rocky path on the summit edge where all competitors met up again.

The roadbook said simply "Summit. BEWARE!" At the summit it felt quite exposed in a strong but deliciously cool wind, not just a breeze. It was great to see each competitor reach this summit and then break into a broad smile as the cool wind buffeted around the rocks before us. It was an amazing feeling and served as a reminder that the heat we'd just experienced coming up the ascent had been increasing rapidly: it was getting to that time of day again.

As I stood taking in the feeling of coolness we all cheered the approaching *Pompiers de Vannes Aventure* (the Firemen from Vannes Adventure). These amazing men had become a popular feature of this year's Marathon des Sables and were met with applause everywhere they went.

And no wonder. The firemen were a team of nine here to complete the Marathon des Sables… carrying a 28 kg, when empty, type of sedan chair with a fixed wheel on the front and handles on the sides, occupied by one of four disabled teenagers (twins Guillaume and Thibault, Mathieu and Victor) with whom the firemen wanted to share this adventure and whom otherwise couldn't. That's a lot of weight to carry, in addition to each fireman's own rucksack weight. The firemen would take turns to carry this heavy chair in six minute stints for the entire 153 miles of the event, with each teenager enduring at least a stage in the desert. It was awe-inspiring to see this. It was just as tough for the four teenagers as the nine firemen, baking as they were in the unforgiving sun and ambient heat.

The firemen and the lucky teenager reached the summit and were met by cheers and tears from pretty much all of us standing there. A couple of the firemen took a rest to cry. I think I shed a tear too at this pure example of selflessness.

I took a last look at the awesome uninterrupted panoramic view before me and descended the narrow path for 200 metres (according to the roadbook) into the furnace. The temperature leaped up almost as soon as I came out of the wind.

A series of "sandy rises" amongst the odd tree and prickly scrub gave way to "a rocky passage by trees" and was increasingly hard work as the hottest time of day approached. I began to worry: this was too hot again. I concentrated on ensuring I was taking enough regular sips rather than gulps of water, ever mindful that Checkpoint 2 was still quite a distance away.

At the top of one of these last "sandy rises" I spotted ahead of me that competitors were hereafter hanging right against the base of some dunes and a *jebel*, before veering left again to meet up directly ahead of me about 1.5 miles away. I figured that following them in a dog-leg fashion was simply adding unnecessary distance and the route straight ahead, while taking in some rolling small sand dunes along the way, had the advantage of a few scrubby bushes and a couple of barren trees with a little shade. It was getting unbearably hot and I was tiring, the thumping headache was coming back along with the feeling of utter weariness, so I took this alternative and apparently shorter route and marched on. As it turned out I was actually taking the correct route, signified by a couple of route marker stakes driven into the sand along the way. A couple of others behind me also saw what I had and chose to do the same. In this way we each were able to pass a dozen or so competitors.

I wondered how and why this long line to my right had decided to follow what looked an odd diversion, but I figured that as soon as one person had decided to do this earlier in the day then many others would simply follow. This wasn't a wise course of action, I thought, in the middle of a desert. True, this small diversion wouldn't really have added much distance but it wouldn't take much in the cauldron of desert heat or a quickly descending sandstorm for problems to arise: I figured that five or 10 minutes longer in the desert before a checkpoint can mean the difference between having had no water for all that time or still sipping on one's last 100 millilitres. Out here, that was a big difference. Blindly following the person in front without checking the roadbook would later catch some out on the Stage 4 long stage.

A couple of times I stopped to crouch in the little shade of a scrubby bush to force on board more water and food before continuing on my way in the burning temperatures. Eventually I began to feel the promise of a building of restrained energy as the heat began to ease and Checkpoint 2 finally came into view. It seemed that as each minute had passed since the start line I was feeling ever stronger.

Checkpoint 2 dispensed just one 1.5 litre bottle of water, yet from here to the finish bivouac was six miles. I found this encouraging. Ahead of me was a flat dry lake. At the end of this, about two miles away, I could see the route disappear between two huge walls of rock, separated by the sandy Maharch Pass which continued between these two walls for about 1.5 miles. The roadbook seemed to then suggest a relatively straightforward run across sand and pebbles for about 2.5 miles to the finish line.

I was starting to feel strong, perhaps better than I had since the start of Stage 1. The previous night's IV drip combined with proper attention to my water intake today and regular intake of food was gradually helping me feel rejuvenated.

Could I run across this completely flat dried lake bed? I felt as though I could, but I also didn't want to ruin the rest of my race and blow up again. I cautioned myself to take it easy, but perhaps start nudging the upper limits of a faster marching pace with a few runs thrown in. Psychologically I was rebuilding myself for a greater effort from here, fairly confident that my body could now take it.

I'd been stood at Checkpoint 2 eating and drinking and chatting with fellow British competitor, Carole, studying the route ahead. We agreed that the worst of the day seemed to be over and the remaining six miles seemed straightforward. She left Checkpoint 2, seemingly fresh as a daisy, a few minutes before I did.

And then I went for it. A fast march with a couple of runs took me to the other side of the dried lake bed in next to no time at all, passing Carole and a trio of competitors who had left Checkpoint 2 a while earlier.

I looked around in awe at my natural surroundings: huge walls of rock rose ahead of me, stretching endlessly to my left (the imposing *Jebel El Mziouda*) and right, looming ever closer as I approached the narrow entrance to the Maharch Pass; the wind was whipping up quite viciously in the distance to my right. What had very shortly before been an uninterrupted view of flat dried lake bed for miles to my right was instead, now about a mile away, blocked by a thick giant wall of airborne sand in a matter of seconds. I quickened my pace by running for a few minutes, interspersed with fast marching to ensure I got off the dried lake bed and into the Maharch Pass before the coming sandstorm hid its entrance.

The sandy Maharch Pass slowed me down. I went with the slower flow rather than try to fight it and took the pace a little easier.

Just ahead I caught sight of Mark's unmistakeable gait and caught up, delighted to see his beaming friendly face. Mark was plugging away, looking strong as ever. We were going at about the same pace and it was great to spend some time to chat.

Mark had left Wayne earlier to crack on as Wayne was having a tough time. Mark asked if I'd been running with or spoken to anyone, surprised that I was able to cover these daily distances with little contact with anyone else. I explained that I'd always liked to run my own pace, that it was easy for me as long solitary Zen-like outings had been my experience throughout the bulk of my training anyway. That's always been the case for me, finding myself either constantly checking my pace, my gait, my foot strike or watching what my heart rate is doing on shorter, faster runs, or on longer journeys revelling in my surroundings and the present rather than dwelling in the past or on the what-ifs, "zoning out", sometimes with music, with half an eye on all my mechanics and statistics.

It was great to talk about our experiences in the event so far, both of us finding the scenery quite amazing, and we reflected on what the race meant for each of us. Having busy lives it felt very unusual to now have so much time to think about the fundamentals of life. When else do those opportunities present themselves? With nothing else to worry about during the week other than sleep, drink, eat and put one foot in front of the other from a start line to a finish line over several hours it is not surprising that so many Marathon des Sables veterans return home with a different approach to life: many blogs and articles testify to this.

While putting the world to rights and enjoying our chat the sandy route became more stony as we approached the Maharch Oasis. I spotted a building over to our right, a *riad*, which appeared to offer the allure of cold drinks. A couple of event vehicles were parked outside. I had my compulsory 200 euros and some Moroccan dirhams and gave some serious thought to taking this opportunity to have something other than water, preferably ice cold. But as Mark pointed out this could attract a hefty time penalty, counting as “outside assistance”. I passed on the idea.

★ ★ ★

With just over three miles to go it felt as if a switch had been flicked on. I suddenly felt fantastic, amazingly energised: I wanted to push some limits and see what it felt like for the remainder of Stage 3. I sped up my fast march and said I’d meet Mark later. I introduced a couple of longer runs mixed in with my fast march. The stony track became one of compacted mud and stone as it passed the *riad* and wound in a squiggly line for a few hundred metres, passing a village solar pump that had been installed on the 21st Marathon des Sables in 2006.

“I’m struggling to keep up with your walking speed mate and I’m running!” It was Mark catching up with me, still beaming. I laughed and began a trot to the finish.

I felt my patience during today's effort was paying off; slowly but diligently I took back 25 places over this last three miles and felt positively buzzing as I was doing so. I crossed the finish line with a huge smile in strong sandy winds, feeling just a little nauseous but absolutely delighted that I was back from yesterday's brink with Stage 3 having been completed safely. I hadn't gone full throttle and still felt well within my limits. My legs felt tired but still very strong.

Mark followed over the line immediately behind me just 15 seconds back. We'd enjoyed our little competitive race, collected our water ration and made our way to the relaxation of our tent.

★★★

After resting a while and with the mid-afternoon moving into the late-afternoon and early evening it was becoming clear we were going to be in for a windswept and sandy night: already the strength of the wind was lifting the sides of the tent and letting in thick blasts of stinging warm sand. By now we'd largely given up on attempts to brush off anything but the thickest of sand piles. We started to gather up rocks and stones from around us to try and hold down the tent edges, with varying success. We asked passing Berbers to hammer back in the iron tent pegs that the wind was now pulling out of the hard stony ground.

My heel pain was returning and I felt the pressure of a new large blister forming underneath the pre-existing bloody mess: great.

I began to hobble in pain over to the Doc Trotters medical tent. In previous years competitors had made complaints about the treatment by Doc Trotters on their battered feet; various internet blogs tell of tales of scalpels cutting a little too deeply or whole layers of skin being removed. This year two methods were available: join the long queue for Doc Trotters to do it or join the shorter queue to collect your own supplies and do it yourself.

I opted for the shorter queue, confident of my self-surgery for blister care. I was handed some swabs, some bright red stinging liquid (an alternative to iodine which did the same job and stained the skin), a small medical sharp, bandages and a pair of blue surgical plastic cover-shoes. Unfortunately as I sat down to attend to the small balloon of liquid at the back of my right heel my leg muscles started going into spasms and painful cramping. The Doc Trotter's medic took pity on me and kindly patched me up; strictly speaking the medics here weren't supposed to be but were taking pity on the several of us finding ourselves incompetent to rearrange our cramping legs into a position that allowed us to administer our own blister surgery.

Professionally patched up I then joined the queue in the communications tent, which by now was thankfully short as competitors went back to their tents in the increasing sand storm. Eventually I got to send my two emails to my wife to add to my blog: an update from yesterday (which of course I was in no fit state to send at the time) and a summary from today.

What I didn't yet know was that my Stage 1 email summary sent after Stage 1 two days ago had disappeared into the ether along with the rest of the bivouac's emails due to a power failure. I also didn't yet know that the system had randomly already sent and delivered my Stage 2 summary email (which talked of my IV drip escapade) but not my Stage 3 summary email.

I then decided to call my wife: it would be great to hear her voice. She couldn't believe it was me, immediately sounding panicked: *What'swrongwhat'shappenedwhereareyou?!?* It took a few minutes for me to convince her that all was much better than it had been, other than we were now in the middle of a sandstorm and it was so damn hot all the time. My Stage 3 email arrived while we were on the satellite phone. We didn't talk for long as the credit I'd bought very quickly ran out, but it was bliss to hear of home.

I hobbled back to the tent. Wayne had arrived, disorientated and slightly out of it, having today had his own IV drip experience and we all agreed his was far more exotic than mine, being dispensed out in the field somewhere under a tree. After Wayne had received his five bags of IV he was summarily dismissed with the words: "Go on then, 18k to go!"

⋆⋆⋆

A severe sandstorm descended for the night. For any tent that hadn't taken the precaution of weighing down the sides with rocks and stones it was an awful night, not ideal before the long-awaited 51 mile long stage, with the canvas on a couple of tents having reportedly blown away into the sky to reveal the panicked occupants.

Sand was enveloping everything and, despite best efforts with Buffs, sunglasses and sleeping bags, breathing some of the fine dust into our aching lungs was unavoidable. This was unpleasant stuff, coating our faces, getting into our hair and into every nook and cranny of our kit. I could feel my lungs feeling a little heavy with several day's worth of sand building in them. Blowing my nose onto the ground was now emitting globules of blood as the sand acted like sandpaper in my nostrils.

Inevitably much of this evening's conversation, aside from the usual banter and recounting of events so far, turned to tomorrow's 51 mile stage. All of us were looking to get the distance covered in one go and crack on through the night to the finish, rather than opt for sleeping along the course or at a checkpoint, and all of us were nervous about it to some degree.

Despite the sandstorm and some pre-Stage 4 nerves I had the best night's sleep I'd had all week... once the storm died down in the early hours. With Tony having sadly but finally left us this evening with his taxi back to Ouarzazate I'd grabbed his space to try and get a quieter night's sleep: with that little extra distance

Ashley's and Mark's snoring then resembled the sound of fireworks rather than grenades going off.

★★★

GARMIN FORERUNNER 310XT STATISTICS FOR STAGE 3

Distance: 21.26 miles
Time: 7 hours, 20 minutes, 43 seconds
Elevation gain: 1511 feet
Calories burnt: 1826
Heart Rate Average: 123 beats per minute
Heart Rate Maximum: faulty reading

OFFICIAL RACE STATISTICS

Stage 3 finish position: 666 of 833 starters
Finish time: 7 hours, 20 minutes, 51 seconds
Stage 3 abandonments: 9

8

Stage 4
Day 1: El Maharch to Jebel El Mraier: 81.5 km/50.9 miles

> *Happiness does not come from doing easy work but from the afterglow of satisfaction that comes after the achievement of a difficult task that demanded our best.*
>
> Theodore Isaac Rubin

Day 1: Wednesday 11 to Thursday 12 April 2012

The longest and toughest stage of every edition of the Marathon des Sables is the Stage 4 ultra-marathon.

The day, or two days for many, every competitor dreads.

This year the Stage 4 ultra-marathon was to cover just short of 51 miles. A strict time limit is imposed of 34 hours, ordinarily more than generous enough if this were a stand-alone one-day race in mild weather. With the race scheduled to start at 8.45 am Wednesday competitors had to cross the finish line no later than 6.45 pm Thursday.

The roadbook maps extended to three pages. Correction: three *fold-out* pages.

The roadbook also mentioned the words "sand" and "dunes", together, and too many times. It also mentioned *jebels*, "BEWARE! Technical descent… ", camel grass (and we knew by now we didn't like camel grass, even more so if it's likely to be crossed in the dark), summits, and "succession of fairly rocky small valleys".

It seemed this year's Stage 4 couldn't be made much more difficult.

But crack this, according to Marathon des Sables lore, and we'd cracked the event.

This was easier said than done when our legs had already carried us with several kilos of rucksack weight over almost 67 miles over the previous three days. What was it going to feel like to add a 51 mile ultra-marathon on a fourth successive day of running? Very, very few on the bivouac knew, this being virgin territory for all but a few of the competitors.

We spoke little in Tent 78, although banter was a-plenty as usual, as we all made our preparations before heading for the start line. Today I could finally feel my rucksack was visibly lighter than at the start of Stage 1, having shed almost two kgs of weight in food over the last three days. I even had some space in it. This meant I would be carrying today 6.6 kg in my rucksack, before adding the 1.4 kg of water I'd be carrying in my water bottles. I was so glad of having pared back as many grammes as I could before leaving the UK.

I was feeling ever better as time passed though I noted that however much I drank I couldn't fully hydrate to a clear colour of urine. This meant I was starting Stage 4 below par on hydration levels, no doubt as were most of the field. So while I felt strong and anticipated a good performance, heat permitting, I still felt I would need to reign in my ambition until nightfall and cooler temperatures. So I intended to stick with a fast march for quite a while, religiously sip my water and keep taking the salt tablets and electrolytes.

Overall, the roadbook was indicating far, far too many stretches of sand and sand dunes for my liking over a 51 mile stage: it was difficult to confirm it from the deceptive impression of the roadbook but I would soon learn that the 15 miles or so from Checkpoint 2 to Checkpoint 4 was pretty much just sand: sand dunes, undulations of sand, or just long stretches of flat, deep sand, the vast majority of which would suck in our weight as we crossed it.

At the start line nervous anticipation electrified the air. We all wished each other the best of luck as the traditional countdown began from 10 seconds and AC/DC's *Highway to Hell* blasted out.

This was truly the stage where that song seemed most appropriate.

The first 6.5 km was a warm-up across a mixture of small sand dunes and a flatter surface of grinding sand and pebbles which didn't help with trying to keep a rhythmic pace. At the end of this, far too soon, we all looked out at the start of a bigger series of sand dunes, bigger than any we had seen thus far. I slowed down significantly: my study of the roadbook for today's stage suggested we'd be coming across plenty of these including what looked to be a 10 km stretch of them later after Checkpoint 4 in what, for those competitors who chose to continue into the night, would be complete darkness.

Although the roadbook suggested this first set of sand dunes after our 6.5 km warm-up lasted for barely a mile it felt like an age to cross them, climbing quite a height before descending again, a cycle repeated for a solid 30 minutes or so. There also seemed to be no crusty surface to them on which to travel firmly; being quite sharp in gradient both on the ascent and descent it really was akin, on the ascents, to travelling up a deep sandy reversed escalator. I felt this starting to get to me and I had to check myself to relax and repeat "*They'll soon be over*" in what was the start of mind-over-matter tricks to get through this stage.

Sure enough I eventually exited these small sand dunes onto rockier ground. My legs were already feeling sapped from the effort I'd just emerged from and we'd only covered five of the 51 miles before us.

I felt more at home on the rocky ground and gently increased my pace, introducing a few runs and consciously walking fast up even the slightest ascent. For quite a few others it was break time, the sand dunes behind us having taken an early toll.

The human snake in front of me disappeared at the foot of the *Otfal Jebel*, which the roadbook stated had a 17% gradient. Picking my way carefully across the boulders, stones and narrow dry *oued* bed I soon reached the foot of the climb. For once the stated gradient seemed accurate until towards the very top but this was one long drag up great flat slabs of rock and boulder, satisfyingly easier to grip and ascend than sand. Was it really just 1 km up this narrow gorge? It didn't feel like it, but accurate distance and time assessment was out of the window in the hot desert conditions where any distance seemed to take twice as long to cover than in the less oppressive environment of home.

The steep rocky walls either side of this narrow boulder-strewn gorge splayed outwards as they rose, acting as an intensifying heat chamber at the narrow base as we climbed up; again I was grateful for the hours I'd spent hoisting myself up moors and hills back home in the UK, my quad muscles seemingly happy with this particular challenge. This was the stuff of hands-on-knees, dig deep, push and drive those legs. Quite a few competitors were struggling and having to take regular rest breaks to catch breath and rest weary legs. To be fair, the vast majority of the Marathon des Sables had thus far been across largely flat or undulating terrain so no one could be chastised for not having done some hilly training. I felt though that, on these hilly sections, I was stronger than many around me for having completed some long hilly runs and walks in my training. I reflected on how much those long sessions and strong quadriceps muscles must have also helped me on the sand dunes thus far, considering that I had not brought walking poles.

No one spoke a word on the long grind upwards to the top of the *Otfal Jebel*. Eventually the narrow rocky walls gradually opened out as the route became steeper still but the sound of hovering helicopters suggested the end was near.

Eventually a few more steps and a turn left to the summit took us out onto possibly the most spectacular panoramic view of the whole event. I could see all around, north, east, west and south-east for miles… to distant thick clouds of a sandstorm. Intermittently the clouds of sand gave way to hills and *jebels* in the far distance, bordering the huge rocky plain below. In the distance I could just pick out far faster competitors, the size of pin-heads, moving ever onwards in the haze to Checkpoint 2. For the umpteenth time in this event I found myself marveling at the natural spectacle gifted before me, unlike anything I'd seen before.

At the summit, gazing beyond, we were all breathing sharply, some uttering profanities at this cruel start to the long Stage 4. *What the hell else lies in store over the next 70 kms*? we wondered.

★★★

The roadbook noted "BEWARE! Technical descent to start then sandy descent with average gradient of over 20%."

I wanted to push on and quickly made my way to the safety rope that competitors were initially using to begin the very steep, technical, rocky descent off this *jebel*.

While rocky at first the steep drop gave way to deep, powdery sand. Being careful to avoid the visible rocks (but forgetful of invisible rocks in the deep sand) I gathered speed as I descended. My left hand reminded my tired brain what it was doing as it began to burn from the friction of continuing to hold onto the rope; letting go I began a visually awkward duck-like gait, pulling up my legs from the deep sand to bring each leg round in front of me in a form of circular motion, my body rocking slightly in sympathy, to plunge in to the deep powder again, sometimes up to my knees. Instinct told me before long that I was dropping too fast; with rockier patches coming up, and yelps from competitors ahead of me who'd found the rocks, I broke my speed a short while before continuing a reckless but exhilarating fast descent in the sand. This was great fun and I arrived at the bottom after several minutes with a big grin on my face, looking back at the long dark channel of disturbed sand marking the route down for those behind me, lemmings in the quest for speed down a seemingly innocuous sandy bank.

With some energy coming back to me, most likely from the adrenaline of excitement, I trotted in to Checkpoint 1 and quickly moved through it after replenishing my water bottles.

★ ★ ★

A few sandy kilometres onwards we came across an incongruous sight: before us lay a flat watery plain dotted by hard mud banks, boulders and stone, the *Rheris oued*. This had to be crossed with care, wet trainers meaning wet shoes and inevitable blisters. Fortunately I'd avoided blisters so far, save for the injury on my right heel, and I didn't want to get any so early in today's stage.

Competitors spread out in an attempt to cross the *Rheris oued*. Some swore loudly as legs slipped in to the pools of water in attempts to cross. Some just ran through the pools seemingly oblivious, which was surely a mistake. I took the opportunity to thoroughly douse my hat in a cool pool and slap it back on to my head, wallowing in the welcome relief as evaporation did its work but far too quickly.

I took my time carefully picking my way across the rocks. I knew almost immediately as my left foot touched what looked to be a sturdy rock that it wasn't. I felt my trainer take on water as it dipped in to a pool fleetingly, before I launched myself onto a larger patch of rock. *Shit*! I thought. It was going to be a long day anyway so I took the precaution of sitting down for a few minutes to dry off my left foot and socks as best I could before putting them on again.

The heat continued to climb on the relatively flat but sandy march to Checkpoint 2. I felt disappointed that the route seemed to be an endless sandy one. The sand gently ascended a good while before a short dip took us into Checkpoint 2; I jogged in with the intention of a rest to get some food on board before the long schlep of over eight miles to Checkpoint 3. Ominously the water ration given here was three litres. I just spotted speed demon Paul and a couple of others heading off as I arrived.

I found a Land Rover just in front of a couple of palm trees. Shade was non-existent. I sat on the metal footplate but this wasn't as comfortable as I'd hoped; I slumped awkwardly, stiffly, onto the sand instead. I carefully filled my water bottles, adding my electrolytes, pouring a little of the water ration over my head. I had been doing this on a few occasions now over the last few days: it was only ever 100 or 200 millilitres (whatever was left after filling my water bottles) and I always reveled in this simple pleasure as an immediate shiver ran from the top of my head and tickled down my neck and upper back. But the constant enveloping heat would ensure this respite didn't last for long: it never ceased to amaze how the cooling feeling would disappear just as quickly as it arrived, in seconds. This act was though one of the many of the MdS that came to symbolise much of what this extreme challenge gave: a series of heightened sensory experiences. This basic act of pouring a little water over my head as I sat by the Land Rover is so etched in my memory I can picture the whole process in minute detail and feel the shiver as I write.

The flies joined me in devouring a Peperami and a few sweets. I'd long since given up waving my hands to shift them. Any that didn't escape in time were just another source of protein. This had been the new normality since Stage 2. Having rested, had a drink and eaten a little I knew I shouldn't continue to sit roasting any longer in the scorching sun and so steeled myself to move off to Checkpoint 3.

I hauled myself up off the sand and got going, my leg muscles thankful for having blood pumping through them again.

On the long stage the top 50 men and top five women do not start until three hours later than the rest of the field. So it was that very shortly after exiting Checkpoint 2 the leading runner bounded past in a jaw-dropping example of running economy and ease.

And he was fast! I'd read before coming out to Morocco that it was a good wheeze to try and keep up with the leading runners for a few metres once they pass to have some idea of the pace they are running across sand. There was absolutely no way I was doing this. I had zero energy in my legs to lift them that much for any length of time and I could see perfectly well in front of me that the leading runners were a marvel at their ability to cross a sandy bog at speed. A number of us slumping along the sand clapped in admiration, a simple hand wave given back in acknowledgement.

As we ate up the next few hundred metres seeing this was both awe-inspiring and dispiriting. How much quicker for them would 51 miles pass... The eventual winner of Stage 4, Salameh Al Aqra, covered the distance in an incredible seven hours and 13 minutes. The original leader we had first seen, Rachid El Morabity (the winner of the 2011 MdS and thus far leader of the 2012 race), lost the lead a crushing just over half a mile from the finish and had to withdraw from the race with an agonising injury: the muscles of his left leg had torn away from the bone.

There seemed to be few people around me not long after leaving the hubbub of Checkpoint 2 and once the leaders had bounded along. Over a 51 mile route the field was already spread out. I could see competitors ahead of me and a few further back. But for all that I could see people I was acutely aware of absolute silence: the sensation of sight yet no sound was oddly surreal. The air was silent and perfectly still: there was no breeze at all as we were now in the blazing cauldron of the day. My own feet made little sound as they pushed forward in the deep soft sand. It felt odd to see movement yet hear nothing: I was sensitive to the sound of my own breathing... but of nothing else. I wallowed in the experience, realising that I'd never before experienced almost true silence.

★★★

Checkpoint 2 was the beginning of almost 16 miles of nothing but sand through to Checkpoint 4 with the odd stony track thrown in. I was to find this very tough.

This was just one huge 16 mile sand pit.

As I grinded along and minutes became hours I found myself becoming steadily despondent. The initially flat but sandy route had become sand dunes giving way to camel grass atop smaller sand bumps and yet more low-lying sand dunes. I was desperate for the next small sandy hill to yield to harder terrain. But it didn't. It is difficult to get across the experience of a continual, unrelenting grind across a terrain of nothing but deep sand and small dunes.

And I'd only absorbed barely four miles since Checkpoint 2.

It was time to break into my reserve for a time just such as this. I had put up an imaginary "Break Glass In Emergency" plastic case around my iPod. Knowing that I still had a long distance of sand to cover, for the first time since the start of the race I plugged in and tried to zone out. This worked, for a short time. I tried to think of anything else except the sand in front and all around me, now starting to torture me with its endlessness.

An inward series of groans (*Why am I here? What am I doing?*) gave way to a more positive interest as the visual scene changed from uninterrupted bumps of sand to a set of ruins: a series of sand dunes before me met a short but sharp ascent up the sand to the ruins of *Ba Hallou* that formed part of the rocky sides of a bowl shape. I could see I would reach the middle bottom of the bowl where a Land Rover sat keeping an eye on approaching competitors. As I neared and then passed the *Ba Hallou* ruins I absorbed as much as I could of this change in scenery: they were impressive. I wondered how long these abandoned buildings had stood here in the middle of nothingness, who had lived there, why and where they had gone.

A brief wind gave some respite from the heat so I broke into a few short runs across a stony track. Team GB endurance athlete, Jen Salter, glided past effortlessly. She gave a wave as I shouted encouragement, bounding off into the distance. The roadbook tells me the route kept the *Rheris oued* to the right while crossing several wooded zones: I remember nothing of these. I was now having a tough time.

Eventually Checkpoint 3 arrived. Another three litres of water were issued, indicating another tough section to come. I was very tired, my legs felt shot and were becoming devoid of any energy. I took a short break to concentrate on getting some food and water into me: the course would now take a turn for the worse, if that were possible, as the roadbook indicated a line of misery and pain through some more imposing sand dunes. In fact, about five miles of them before the route became apparently easier in the run-in to Checkpoint 4. By the time I would arrive there it would be getting dark with still some 20 miles to go.

This section of sand dunes was the only point in the whole event where I wished I'd brought walking poles. I'd bought some light-weight poles in the week or two before I left home; I decided two days before leaving not to bring them in an effort to keep my overall rucksack weight down. As the sand dunes repeated themselves and became steeper a few people overtook me with walking poles. However, descending the other side of the dunes meant I wasn't hampered by a couple of sticks and I simply caught up and overtook those people again. This cat-and-mouse game continued for several miles. In my mental fug I became slightly annoyed that I couldn't pass them and stay ahead. An organiser's sand buggy roared past us several times, checking for competitors who had keeled over in the steep dunes, the driver and his companion beaming huge smiles: *now that looks fun!* I thought, tinged ever so slightly with resentment at how easy some others had it. Eventually five miles of sand dunes had become just one sand dune more and I finally built a clear gap to those behind me now encumbered by their walking poles.

I tried to think of other things.

★★★

My legs aching, my mouth parched, these dunes spat me out to a steep bank of sand ahead of me which took me to the crest of *Jebel Lahnoune*. I could just catch a darkening glimpse of the panoramic view ahead of me but dusk became complete darkness in a surprisingly few minutes.

As I reached the exposed crest what had been oppressive still heat for hours gave way to the surprise of a very strong gale; sand was being whipped up in ferocious clouds that stung my exposed legs, hands and head. I needed to move quickly to Checkpoint 4 as it was clear a nasty sandstorm was closing in. I thought I spotted some race officials at the bottom of this small sandy *jebel* and remembered the roadbook making it clear that head torches and glow stick had to be attached and turned on by dusk… and was there a time penalty for non-compliance? I couldn't think straight to remember. Quickly, I stopped, removed my rucksack from an aching back, broke my glow stick and attached it to the back of my rucksack to guide those behind me (I hoped I wouldn't get lost overnight), switched on my head torch and did my best to cover my exposed head with my Buff, lessening the stinging of the vicious airborne swirls of sand.

Suitably lit up I descended the sandy rocky drop to meet something resembling a track. Finally out of the sand it took a few minutes to get back into the swing of running and walking; the stony, rocky, lumpy track was lethal and a hasty step would wreck ankles. I kept half an eye on a couple of competitors ahead of me to guide my way more safely. Further along the track I could see a meandering line of a few glow sticks snaking its way towards a collection of lights glowing dimly in the sandy air. At last! Checkpoint 4 was now in view. I'd broken the back of this day. I had no intention of stopping and wanted to plough on overnight until I finished, whenever that would be.

I arrived at Checkpoint 4. The atmosphere was palpably gloomy. Sand was everywhere, filling the air, enveloping everything and impossible to get away from, except for the two officials looking thoroughly miserable as they sheltered in their Land Rover. I could barely see more than a few metres in front of me. A couple of masked officials noted my number and gave me my 1.5 litre water ration; saying nothing, an outstretched arm guided me through the dark to where, I guessed, I should go to collect myself before continuing.

Checkpoint 4 was eerily quiet. I could see numerous people, a few vehicles, some tents, but heard nothing aside from what was now a howling wind and the sound of sand smacking against vehicles, canvas and me. The couple of tents I could see were already full: one a medical tent occupied by the wounded; another taken up by prostrate competitors looking completely hacked off, knackered.

There wasn't anywhere else for me to go other than balance myself on the uncomfortable metal step by the door of a Land Rover, gradually allowing myself to be covered in a film of the thick whirling sand. Sat next to me were two American competitors: she sounded completely done in, fed up. She asked her companion if they should plough on through the night.

How long would it take?

Wouldn't it be okay to rest a while longer?

How can we continue in this sand?

I'm so sore… I'm really tired…

He could barely utter much in response, quietly contemplating his own exhausted state.

I was by now crunching my way through my dinner, a second helping for the day of a cold breakfast cereal, crunchy oat granola this time with rehydrated milk powder. I gagged on the first spoonful as I took in a generous dollop of airborne sand too. But I got used to it. It was impossible to eat without sand being introduced to the nutritional equation. I finished off my cereal and washed everything down with gulps of water, spitting out the first mouthful to clear my mouth of gritty particles of damn sand.

It had been dark now for about an hour. It was time to move on, away from the negative conversation sat beside me. Refuelled, I got ready for travelling with just my head torch to guide me across the blackness. Across yet more sand dunes.

★ ★ ★

I couldn't see it as yet but a bright green laser beam should have been streaking across the sky from Checkpoint 5 to the checkpoint I was now stood in: the whirling sands in the air were hiding it from view.

By now, having been sat a short while, I was cold, the energy-sapping heat giving way to an increasingly cold air: I now put on my spare T-shirt under my long-sleeved top, put my cap and Buff back on and headed towards a narrow exit channel marked by opposite glowing wooden sticks driven into the sand. These showed the way out of the gloom of Checkpoint 4 and onwards into apparent nothingness.

Stood at the entrance to this channel looking ahead into the dark I switched my head torch back on: the roadbook told me I needed to take a 70 degree compass bearing to Checkpoint 5. I was keen to keep following my compass bearing which I now took to the first small green glow stick a few metres in front of me. I intended to rely on the compass bearing and ignore any other guiding glow sticks. I jogged away from Checkpoint 4.

Over the coming miles it became clear many before me had instead sought to rely solely on the glow sticks which had been struck into the sand seemingly haphazardly along the way. I noticed the odd sight of the head torches of other competitors that were visible up to a mile away to either side of me. How did that happen? I checked my compass: I was still on the right bearing. What I later learnt was that the local children (where were they from? how did they get here? how did they get back?) had run off with several of the glow sticks along the course or moved them around randomly. Bless 'em.

It took me a while to adjust to the unnerving sense of being surrounded by a void of blackness, except for my head torch's beam of white light in front of me. It felt weird, my whole sensory world seemingly nothing other than that tunnelled beam ending in a white circle in front of me. At first I had to switch off my head torch for a few seconds to allow my brain to adjust, for it to know that there were still in fact different sights around me, different shapes and inclines. As the night wore on and I became increasingly exhausted, it seemed to gradually affect my eyes after hours spent focussing on that white tunnelled beam and small white circle.

The first time I switched off my head torch I stood and marvelled at what only a desert sky could offer: zero light pollution. I stood and dreamily breathed "*Wow!*" as I took in from the sky above me almost a solid carpet of glowing stars of varying subtle shades of whiteness and size. It was truly amazing. I cracked on for a while without my head torch on, soaking in this natural marvel enjoyed all the more by the fact I could neither see nor hear any soul around me: there was complete and utter silence. It was difficult though to stick to my 70 degree compass bearing in the dark so I reluctantly returned to keeping my head torch on.

Having jogged a while up and down some smaller sand dunes I was before long overheating from the second layer I had put on at Checkpoint 4. Dropping my rucksack I stripped off my upper half, enjoyed the brief respite of cooler night air, and put my long-sleeved top back on. I then tried to take my 70 degree compass bearing again… *where's my compass?!*

I panicked, I felt a surge of urgent adrenalin as I hyperactively looked around me, checked my body, checked my rucksack… *Where's my damn compass?*

Something like this wouldn't normally be something to worry about, but I'd come to rely on it through the race and now it was lost. I could suffer a time penalty for this. More seriously, I was in the middle of a huge field of sand dunes in the pitch black with no-one around me… *without my compass.*

A good five minutes passed as hours as I desperately searched for it, even digging my hands into the sand around me trying to find it… until common sense reminded me that wasn't a good idea: scorpions, snakes and camel spiders have to sleep somewhere.

Phew! Finally I found it, wrapped in the T-shirt I'd just taken off. It was a long five minutes searching. My panicked over-reaction was unlike me, a sign of my very tired, addled state.

I jogged and marched onwards through the rising and sinking dunes in the far cooler, but still warm, night-time air. Time wore on.

Along the course I came across a prostrate competitor lying by the side of a dune.

My first thought, oddly, was whether he was dead, was he okay?

I slowed my pace as I passed. He *looked* comfortable, wrapped up in his sleeping bag, head barely peaking out of the top, resting on his rucksack. In the middle of nowhere. In the dark. With desert nasties looking for somewhere warm to sleep… a warm-blooded being, ideally… in a sleeping bag…

"Are you OK?" I asked.

No response.

"*Ca va?*"

Again, no response.

"How are you feeling?"

Still nothing,

I decided, perhaps illogically as I didn't get a reply, that he wasn't dead and jogged on. I figured at the time that someone who had gone to the effort of getting wrapped up into a sleeping bag probably just wanted to sleep without being asked questions by dozens of passing competitors. I also remembered our British liaison official explaining to us (was it yesterday morning?) that we would be allowed to sleep alongside the course during the night stage, a relaxation of the normal rule that this was only allowed at the checkpoints. So I felt pretty sure he hadn't passed on to the great ultra-marathon in the sky.

★ ★ ★

Yet more sand dunes passed with time.

Then really quite weird things started to happen.

I was marching at a pace when, outside of my torch light in my peripheral vision, a large owl flew past me barely a few metres ahead. I think. An owl? In the middle of the desert? I'm still not entirely sure.

Further on I tread softly as a pristine white lamb, sitting comfortably in the sand, a tiny thing barely a couple of weeks old, didn't seem too fussed that I was coming near it. It wasn't, because it didn't exist: as I was almost on top of this pristine white lamb the pristine white lamb became a pristine bump of sand just outside of the glow of my head torch.

I did though come across the pristine white canvas sides of a Berber tent, complete with thick guy ropes holding it in the sand.

I vividly recall beginning to move sideways away from it as I approached, not wanting to disturb the sleeping occupants… until instead I just ran, smiling to myself, up and over what it was: a series of large sandy bumps of camel grass atop a sand dune.

None of this felt unnerving at the time and felt perfectly ordinary; I saw these things as real as the pages of this book. I smiled to myself and shook my head: "*Weird!*", I thought.

I've since learnt that, without much in the way of visual or auditory stimulation, I was going through a mild form of hypnagogic hallucinations or illusions: I was falling asleep on my feet in my exhausted state, my brain veering between sleep and wakefulness, confusing the real and the imagined, stumbling around in a half-sleep.

This shouldn't have been surprising considering I hadn't slept more than a few hours for the last several nights while exercising to extremes during the day. And I felt utterly whacked. Not having anyone around me probably didn't help either: it seemed I were the only person around for miles.

More food seemed to be the answer: I tucked in to my 50 gramme bag of Rowntree's Sour Faces, devoured in seconds. It wasn't long before I started feeling much better, and more awake.

In fact, much, *much, MUCH* better!

How do I describe what happened not long after this point?

A bolt from the sky had jolted life into me. *I was alive!!!!!!* Beaming, smiling, laughing, a switch had been thrown and I felt brimming with energy.

I could *run*! Having negotiated a series of smaller sand dunes to come across the tops of larger ones, I could now see and follow the intense streak of a solid green laser beam coming from Checkpoint 5, scoring unmistakeably across the sky above me and back towards Checkpoint 4.

My vision seemed to clear now. I could see the large structure that was emitting the green laser beam, and it was getting closer! I finally reached it, a Moroccan army soldier emerging from the military vehicle housing the beam atop a large mound; his outstretched arm pointed me towards the arc lights of Checkpoint 5.

I was still running! A few competitors had somehow missed the home of the laser beam, trying to pick their way from either side of me across the stony plain to Checkpoint 5: their head torches flashed towards me as they caught my beam gunning for the checkpoint. A competitor to my right was off in the distance, in danger of overshooting the parallel of Checkpoint 5; he realised his error having seen my head light moving away from him towards the lights of the Checkpoint and he got back on track.

My competitive streak was coming back. I increased my pace.

A whoop of cheers and clapping rose as my GPS timing chip activated the bleep when I crossed the mats at Checkpoint 5.

I looked around to see who the cheers were for.

"Way to go Mark! You look awesome!"

I hadn't realised it was for me! I stopped with a beam on my face, feeling fantastic. A couple of the *controlleurs* remarked how strong I was looking, which boosted me further. I didn't want to stop: I took on board a few more sweets and swigged down plenty of water. I didn't hang around and moved off from Checkpoint 5, a number of competitors huddled in the tents looking over to see who this hyperactive runner was.

Where was this coming from? Twelve hours ago I had started and it had been a largely miserable slog. I now found myself hardly walking at all. I felt fresh, strong, cool. How I felt now was far, far removed from how I felt strung up to an intravenous drip just two days ago, or how exhausted I felt barely a few hours beforehand.

Pain? What was that? I felt completely free of all pain after 12 hours: I felt strength in my legs, I felt invincible. *This felt so easy!*

It was the highest of runner's highs I've ever experienced. The almost seven miles from Checkpoint 5 to Checkpoint 6 passed in no time at all. I passed dozens of struggling competitors, some barely able to stand up: they looked completely demoralised as I bounded past with a joyous "*Bonjour!*"

If only I could have bottled this feeling. I felt truly fantastic. The terrain felt easy and I was bounding along. An almost straight line was taking me now to the lights of Checkpoint 6! I was also now listening to invigorating music on my iPod. As I neared the marshals at the entrance to Checkpoint 6 they began to look very concerned: approaching them was an apparently unhinged guy full of beaming smiles and greetings. The other marshalls looked like as you'd expect: bored, tired and slightly fed up after too many hours stood at a checkpoint.

I recognised one of the first *controlleurs* as the guy who looked very alarmed when I got off the coach on bivouac arrival day with my desperate pained look of "I really need the toilet!" He had now that same worried expression, perhaps confusing my grinning look of glee for that similar pained expression, fearing I hadn't yet recovered and was going to explode all over him and Checkpoint 6. But he soon seemed to relax and my enthusiasm must have been infectious: the other *controlleurs'* body language and quizzical expression moving from an initial askance "*What the hell is this guy on?!*" to comradely beaming smiles.

"You feeling good?"

"Definitely! I feel great!" I replied.

I gulped down more water and ploughed on quickly, not resting long at all.

A fraction over 6.5 miles now stood between me and the end of this 51 mile stage. I didn't know where this burst of energy was coming from but I wanted to exploit it as much as I could while it lasted. I ran on, shuffling almost silently in the sand, a sandy *oued* bed according to the roadbook, past competitors aching along with walking poles.

An area of sand bumps and camel grass slowed me down for a

short while before I regained some speed across a stony plain. *I was still alive!* I took on a few more sweets for the final push.

Then I could see it: the bright shining lights of the finish bivouac in the distance.

The race was on! I could hear a few other competitors that I'd recently passed now gaining on me, trying to reel me in. I could hear their loud laboured breathing and figured they wouldn't be able to keep up if I pushed just a little harder still: I felt strong; this didn't feel an effort anymore. I gathered a few extra seconds per mile of pace and pushed on, the laboured breathing behind me falling away to become whispers of breath before that sound was replaced with the soft rasp of a breeze moving through the camel grass.

Just as the undulating sandy bumps and camel grass were getting harder work, stinging the bare skin of my legs, the terrain gave way to flat terrain with pebbles. I was now on a track, easy to run on. A competitor ahead of me looked around, he now hearing my laboured breathing bearing down on him.

He veered left, continuing down the track. I could see the bivouac lights clearly now, but to get to them I would need to take a sharp right across the stony ground and deviate off the track. Why did he veer left? Had he seen something I hadn't that more indicated the line to the finish?

I couldn't see it. I ran on, turning sharply right off the track. Half a mile to the finish. I looked left and saw my competitor looking visibily peeved; he tried to put on a greater pace to catch me but I wasn't having that. It gave me another boost of adrenalin and I ran on harder again, burning him off: he slowed instead to a walk, realising he wasn't, after all these hours, going to hold off the loss of another place… not that it mattered in the general scheme of things.

My legs opened up and I was cruising, or at least that's what it felt like. After 18 long hours I crossed the line to a few claps and "Well done!" from the *controlleurs.*

And then, having stopped, I felt sick.

This time I managed to keep my stomach contents in place. I took a few sips of sweet Moroccan tea, collected my 4.5 litres of water and then ever so slowly hobbled around in the disorientating dark to find Tent 78: it was difficult to get my bearings and work out what was where.

Most of my tent mates had returned, just one or two were left to come in. I had a few quick words with Paul and Richard: anybody else was either asleep, too spaced out to speak or still on the course. I couldn't see so didn't know.

It was by now somewhere around 3 am Thursday morning. I'd been on the move since 8.45 am Wednesday morning. My legs had carried me 51 miles today across some tough terrain in the ever-present heat. Almost as quick as it had arrived the excitable abundant energy that had appeared somewhere around mile 38 was now fast draining away. I felt sleepy. I didn't feel hungry yet my waist pouch still contained a lot of the food I'd planned to eat over this stage. Having seen Stage 4 through to the finish overnight I knew I had the rest of Thursday to try and recover. With the hardest stage completed I dared to think I'd cracked the race.

It seemed too much of an effort to pluck my sleeping bag out of my rucksack and change into my evening T-shirt and shorts. So I didn't.

Barely 15 minutes after I arrived back at Tent 78 I crashed back onto the hard comfort of my rucksack, out for the count. Apparently it threw it down with rain in the early hours of the morning (in the Sahara?!): I must have been completely out of it as I didn't notice a thing.

9

Stage 4: Day 2

I attempt an arduous task; but there is no worth in that which is not a difficult achievement.

Ovid

Thursday 12 April 2012

After my ultra-marathon effort I'd slept soundly for a solid six hours. It still wasn't enough, as I woke up feeling tired, but it felt like I'd slept the best I had in days.

The climbing heat of the day bearing down on the black canvas of our tent and the burning brightness of the sun had woken me up around 9.30 am. It began to feel as though I were in a boil-in-a-bag, slowly cooking. I quickly unzipped out of my sleeping bag and realised three things.

Firstly, I didn't need to run or walk any distance today (other than to Doc Trotters). Having continued through the night to finish the 51 mile stage that started at 8.45 am yesterday I had the joy of knowing today was a rest day for me. While competitors had been finishing throughout the night dozens upon dozens were still out on the course, gradually being sapped yet again by the ever-present heat and burning sun of the day.

Secondly, I knew I was dehydrated. Very dehydrated. I would need to make sure I sipped my water regularly throughout today to try and get topped up. There were still 36 miles to go to the finish line of this race.

Thirdly, my right foot was a mess. The nasty blister I had picked up on the Grantham Ultra a few weeks ago was not best served by having run and walked 118 miles over the last four days. A few smaller blisters on my left foot were letting me know they were there, but they were only a tiny irritant compared to the mess on my right heel, a bloody, sandy raw hole oozing liquid. At some point today I'd visit Doc Trotters again.

Overall I felt a low level throb of aches in my legs: the desert heat and lots of lying around on a sleeping bag over the last few days after each stage had combined to keep the general pain level low. It was only on standing and having to move around that the analgesic effect of simply lying down in the heat doing nothing disappeared in a flash.

Today was another of those days when I would be immersed in the experience of being disconnected from pretty much everything: it was quiet, with no emails or phones to deal with; there became very little to do other than think and contemplate the immediacy of my surroundings, gaze at the hazy desert scenery and review the much shrunken contents of my rucksack.

I took a leisurely breakfast. All of us in Tent 78 moved around gingerly, tell-tale hobbles and odd bodily jerks giving signs of where our injuries lay.

The morning passed luxuriously, lounging around in our tent watching and clapping other finishers as they, many hours since the start of the stage, passed by our tent as a caravan of shattered, energised, joyous, dejected finishers of the toughest stage of this event.

Rich and Wayne were in top form as we all exchanged stories and jokes about the day and night before. We all felt quietly confident that the bulk of the race was now cracked, but Mark's wiser view was that the race was far from over yet.

Around lunchtime we heard that the final competitor was approaching the finish line. A few of us wandered over to see in the fake last finisher. He looked quite confused and then delighted as he approached a small crowd clapping and cheering on the finish line. But worryingly the organisers had got the numbers wrong and there were still others out on the course: the last finisher was still quite a while away.

As I was now up and about, albeit walking strangely as my tight legs and blisters refused to co-operate to allow me to move fluidly, I figured now was the time to visit Doc Trotters for my heel blister.

A long queue. The odd laugh permeated the air. Otherwise we stood quietly exchanging war stories of the night before, marvelling at the long desert vista, or remained silent. A thick sand storm was gathering: it was time to cover my face with my Buff as the airborne sand became thick. I was stood in a loose pair of shorts, my bare legs getting shot-blasted by sand. Some considered this discomfort more unpleasant than whatever injuries they were queuing for Doc Trotter treatment and left, hobbling ungainly towards the slightly better comfort of their tents.

This meant I moved up the queue quicker but I realised as I neared the entrance that this was some kind of triage tent. Competitors had a choice: note down your name with an official to join the main Doc Trotters' tent queue a short walk away; or stay here to be dispensed with whatever you needed to treat your own injuries: Doc Trotters' staff were handing out scalpels and various medical paraphernalia to those who couldn't face another queue.

That included me. I really didn't want to queue yet again. I decided to try a do-it-yourself approach and took possession of a piece of blue plastic, a scalpel blade, small phials of anti-septic eosin and various plasters and other bits and pieces that I might need.

I found a space on the sandy floor and poured a phial of non-stinging eosin on my heel. A sickly red-stain remained. I tried to hold the scalpel blade in my left hand and contort my right arm and right leg into a position which meant I could pierce the watery, bloody ball on the outside of my right heel, itself sat under the raw exposed skin of my older blister. I nicked it, but my stiffness wasn't making this easy: a trickle of blood and clear fluid pooled on to the blue plastic… and then I started to cramp. I could barely move.

This was going to take a while.

This now explained the constant queue for what should have been a quick process: several of us were on the floor of the tent in what must have been a day-long procession of competitors in various painful contortionist moves trying to self-medicate, groans and the odd expletive peppering the air. If you didn't know any better you'd think you were looking in at an extreme yoga class. Now I noticed that the Doc Trotters staff were taking pity and, rather than simply continuing to hand vicious implements to amateurs or take names onto a list for the main medical tent, were gradually working around us to slice, patch and dispense.

The doctor who dealt with me was very efficient: she cut, sliced, drained, applied more eosin, issued instructions and tape, put on a blue plastic shower shoe and sent me on my way.

I emerged into the air which was again thick with sand. I struggled to see with sand stinging my eyes: my Buff could only cover so much and my sunglasses were in my rucksack in our tent.

My heel, now open to the elements except for the blue plastic shoe I was now wearing, was really quite painful. It was almost on the verge of agony. I could barely walk in a proper fashion as it was and now I was struggling to put one leg in front of the other for the couple of hundred metres I desperately wanted to cover to reach Tent 78.

It took an age. My pained gait meant I had to stop every few metres to empty out the sand from my sandals and try and hold my feet in them, quite difficult when one of them is sporting a blue plastic shower shoe.

Finally I made it. It had been quite an exhausting effort. I slumped onto my bag, after emptying it and myself of the sand that had deposited absolutely everywhere and on everything in the sandstorm. The weather remained unsettled: the winds were strong.

Then stopped.

The temperature seemed to plummet. It was getting cold.

The boom of a crack of thunder? Another?

Sure enough, in the hottest desert in the world, we were experiencing a thunderstorm. Hail fell thickly, small balls of ice bouncing off the parched desert floor. We couldn't believe it and felt for the competitors still out on the course who would now be wet, freezing cold and suffering immensely.

The thunder and hail storm stopped after about ten minutes. All returned to normal. A Berber later explained that this never used to happen in the hottest desert on Earth.

Another ten minutes later and the sandy atmosphere had settled, the sky was clear, the sun bore down: it was scorching once again.

* * *

Mark mentioned with a big smile that apparently we would all be getting an ice cold can of Coke later.

We were like giddy kids at Christmas.

"Really?" I asked. "Are you sure?"

I'd heard about this momentous event in my pre-Marathon des Sables reading and had completely forgotten about it. To think! Something other than water warmed in the shadow of Land Rovers to 40C, with a taste of High 5 Zero electrolytes, the Orange flavour I was now finding to be making me feel sick.

"Yep, we hand in our race numbers for fresh new ones in exchange for a cold can of Coke!"

Mark was beaming now, delighted to be the one spreading the news. Like a bunch of teenage boys forever grateful to Mark for having shown us the hole in the wall of the women's changing room at the local swimming baths, we beamed back at Mark, the wise one, the giver of this amazing image.

It was a stark difference: an ice cold can of fizzy Coke versus six days of too-warm water. We analysed everything about this future momentous event. We discussed and began to doubt the Coke would be ice cold: how can it be in the hottest desert in the world? We imagined and spoke excitedly about pulling the ring pull on the can and hearing the crack and fizz of *cold, sugary goodness!*

This momentous forthcoming event became the main event of the day. It may be hard to imagine for any reader not having been through such extremes as the Marathon des Sables to comprehend the significance of something so commonplace. But, for us, sat reeking (we presumed: we couldn't tell), aching, injured, going through various phases of personal revelation, the simplistic act of cracking open an ice cold can of Coke took on almost religious significance.

"Are you going to save it for later or drink it as soon as you get it?" asked Mark.

We all thought long and hard on that one. Some might save it; some would gulp it in one go. Most of us were going to take an age over drinking it, savouring the temporary lift of something just so *icy cold*.

In the midst of this discussion, lazing around, staring out to the sands, we looked across to the middle of the bivouac and saw a group of officials assembling. A crowd quickly formed and quickly dispersed, new clean race numbers in hand with that cold can of fizz.

Mark, Paul, Ash and I decided to wander over, the crowds having dispersed by now. In the ceremony we handed over filthy race numbers and received in exchange clean ones (for the benefit of the sponsors who would see us out on the course the next day) and… yes… an ice cold can of Coke. It was the smaller size of a can you'd be given as a complementary on a flight, but ice cold nonetheless.

Walking back to our tent Paul reminded us of the scene from the Second World War film *Ice Cold in Alex*, a true story about a British army crew attempting to drive and push their ambulance across the North African Western desert to the safer British lines. The lead character Captain Anson is motivated by the thoughts of an ice cold lager he will order when reaching their final destination in Alexandria, Egypt (hence the "ice cold" and "Alex" in the title of the film). Apparently, by now having lost several pounds in the last few days, I looked similar to Captain Anson. I had to confess I hadn't seen the film. Paul was mortified. I promised I would look out for it.

Back at our tent we each cradled our precious gift, it still feeling cold. It now assumed biblical proportions of relevance.

The sound of a reassuring crack and a fizz worked its way through our tent. The cold fizz tickling the mouth and throat was delicious and lifted our spirits no end. Odd, considering it was just a small can of Coke, but what was a commonplace had become a thoroughly enjoyable and more intense experience during a week of warm, electrolyte-infused water.

★★★

The rest of the day was spent simply chilling, relaxing, stretching out, tending aches and pains, patching blisters, clapping in the few that were left to finish.

The last finisher came in at around 3.15 pm Thursday: Ah Chew Yee, competitor number 786 of Malaysia, at 74 years of age, was the 801st finisher having walked for some 30 hours painfully across the finish line to a cheering crowd and a welcome hug from race director Patrick Bauer. His endurance had carried him through an incredible 31 hours, 24 minutes and 53 seconds. But sadly he failed to finish the Marathon des Sables, abandoning on the following day's Stage 5.

★★★

Today I had had plenty of time to think, as I had during the Stages I'd already completed. We'd only been away from the Westernised version of civilisation for barely a week but we'd all quickly forgotten the glut and ease of access to pretty much anything after just a few days of very basic living in the desert. How simple it now was to just have to think about getting up, eating a bit, get from position A to position B, eat a bit along the way, eat at the end, and sleep.

Now, a small fizzy can of alternative refreshment had become an icon for appreciating simple experiences. I recalled the thought I'd had somewhere in the dunes on the previous night as I battled through the 51 miles of Stage 4: *when I get back home*, I'd thought excitedly to myself, *I'm going to simply sit and take the time to read a great book*. I've always had a keen interest in reading but this thought oddly felt a new revelation in the desert's cool night air.

All the preparation for this event and now passing daily through its trials and natural wonders was becoming something of grander importance: the sands weren't simply scouring our physical being, they seemed to be scouring the detritus of our cluttered minds.

Lazing around in our tent gazing at the scenery around me I wondered: having come this far in training for and undertaking "the toughest footrace on Earth", what more could I do? What was stopping me? Not just in physical achievements, but in all spheres of my life? My career as a lawyer hadn't been enjoyable for the last couple of years, the combined result of a role that was seemingly designed to become dull with too many hours expected for comparatively poor reward. Why was I continuing something I no longer found enjoyable? What was the point?

Before I came out to the Sahara I'd been watching a recording of an ITV programme about the 23rd Marathon des Sables in 2008. The programme centred on Rory Coleman and another competitor, David Cooke, as they progressed through the race. During the programme, relaxing after a day's hard effort, Rory reflects on David's achievement:

"I think he'll go away and consider life differently. It changes everyone. Everyone that's been here, it always changes them."

At the time of watching it I recall thinking: "*Really? Why?*" It was easy to see it as over-dramatic programming: surely there's just the undoubted pain and hard work of the event and then it's back home to life and recovery... isn't it?

But now I began to understand as I began to experience a change for myself. With no conscious effort this extreme experience was giving to me a keener, sharper awareness of seemingly everything: what really mattered, what it felt like, and what was important.

Being here in the desert, swapping stories and thoughts about all sorts of things with my tent mates, I began to see that this experience, both the race itself and the three years gradually building up to it, was a catalyst for something else.

It was something I'd not, in the waning light of the evening, yet fully thought out. But it did indicate an irreversible new freedom and a rising above the norm to think and do whatever it was I really wanted to do.

★ ★ ★

GARMIN FORERUNNER 310XT STATISTICS FOR STAGE 4

Distance: 50.09 miles
Time: 18 hours, 24 minutes, 49 seconds
Elevation gain: 3278 feet
Calories: 4913
Heart Rate Average: 124 beats per minute
Heart Rate Maximum: faulty reading

OFFICIAL RACE STATISTICS

Stage 4 finish position: 480 of 824 starters
Finish time: 18 hours, 24 minutes, 47 seconds
Stage 4 abandonments: 23

10

Stage 5: Jebel El Mraier to Merdani: 42.2 km/26.2 miles

All limits are self imposed.

Icarus

Friday 13 April 2012

I knew I had done a good job in rehydrating myself the previous day when I found myself really having to summon the energy to get up during the cold night and venture out into the blackness to urinate.

It was freezing cold. I crawled out of my sleeping bag as quietly as I could, the rest of Tent 78 and the bivouac silent (apart from the snores), and shivered. And kept on shivering.

It was about 3 am, the final hour or so before light would start to appear at the horizon. I shivered and hobbled (ah, yes, my painful heel blister reminded me it was still there...) a random indirect walk a suitable distance away from the tent, trying to avoid like a minefield the numerous tell-tale dark patches of dozens of other urine deposits.

I reached the undoubted British-zone of urinating: a respectful, quiet, acceptable distance away from the tents, unlike the French-zone of urinating: in your face, too close, impersonal. It had become a standing joke that the French seemed to delight on moving barely a few metres away from the outer ring of the bivouac predominantly occupied by the British. As the week had wore on the odd groans and words of annoyance from the British had become louder as tolerance wore thin of French competitors noisily urinating in close proximity (and view) of British sensitivities.

Satisfied at my distance away from the tents I switched on my head torch and stood patiently: it wasn't long before the discomfort of a full bladder began to give way to relief.

I saw a small movement on the ground to my left. A terrifying-looking jet black scorpion scurried into the circle of light given off by my head torch.

It was big.

Not wanting to be covered in a pour of human urine it instead started scurrying towards my feet. I wondered if scorpions could jump about three feet into the air with their claws flailing around aimlessly: I didn't want to be standing around too long taking a pee to find out.

This wasn't good. I took a few steps back, not knowing if directing my flow on to the scorpion was a good move or not. I decided it wasn't. The scorpion had gone. I desperately tried to remember where I'd heard that the smaller scorpions were more dangerous or poisonous than the bigger ones, or had I got that the wrong way round or was I thinking of a different creature entirely?

The scorpion scurried back into my circle of light and again towards my feet. Panicked, I stopped peeing. The scorpion stopped in the light. I stopped. I moved sideways, trying to rid myself of this poisonous monster. It followed, at an alarmingly agile speed.

Shit.

This merry little dance couldn't have lasted more than a minute or so but must have looked odd to anyone watching from the comfort of the tents: some bloke dancing around madly in little circles around his torch light for no apparent reason. *The heat's really got to that guy's head…*

Maybe it was following the tiny amount of heat given off by

my light? In nanoseconds I was working out whether or not it was a great idea to switch off my head torch.

I took the risk.

Nothing happened. My eyes took too long to adjust to the absence of light I'd had for several minutes and there I was stood in the now pitch black darkness of the desert with a large scorpion somewhere in my midst.

Tentatively I finished relieving myself, turned, and gingerly stepped my way back towards Tent 78. I dared not switch on my head torch for fear of giving a landing light for the scorpion to follow me back to Tent 78 and take refuge in someone's running shoes or rucksack.

The tent I arrived at didn't look like the one I'd left. I whispered, asking if this was Tent 78. Two doors up, was the whispered reply. I found myself back in my sleeping bag, still shivering, and struggled to get back to sleep to the imagined scuttling of scorpions scurrying across the sand inches above my head.

★★★

The morning before a stage start had now become ritualistic: get up, eat, repack rucksack, apply tape to prone areas, apply sunscreen, collect water, dispense water, walk as a group to the start line.

I still hadn't reached full hydration, the colour of my urine this morning displaying that medical fact. I also had now a constant sore, heavy chest and the odd bloody nose: sand was in my airways on an almost permanent basis now.

Although we were all battle weary and shattered there was now a feeling that we were now on the home straight. Our rucksacks finally felt noticeably lighter, the toggles and straps needed to be tightened to take up the spare room that was now in them. The long stage of 51 miles had been conquered. All that stood in our way between here and a finisher's medal at the finish line and a hug from Patrick Bauer was today's marathon (pah! what's a marathon now?) and the Dreaded Dune Day, Stage 6, to the finish.

But this still had to be given respect. We were warned again that today was going to be very hot and we should take water regularly. Happy Birthday was sung to those who wouldn't be eating birthday cake today and AC/DC's *Highway to Hell* thumped out of the loudspeakers for the countdown. We poured, or rather in our exhausted state, dripped across the start line. The roar of the helicopter close above us elicited for the fifth day excited shouts, roars and screams.

Just over three miles from the start the line of competitors disappeared from the rocky plateau, with other competitors reappearing a little further ahead; they seemed to be scrambling up from a ravine. Sure enough the roadbook highlighted the obstacle: "BEWARE! Large crevasse in oued bed. Technical passage."

Striped red and white tape signalled the start of a queue of competitors before they dropped steeply a good three or four metres to the base of the crevasse and a flat sandy piece of ground alongside a flowing river. Some waited patiently to step across the couple of metres over some hastily-placed vegetation, which was now looking precariously loose and waterlogged. As I and others stood at the top of the crevasse assessing a better way to cross one or two competitors slipped in: more blisters would appear for them.

Taking a short cut a few of us slipped down the sandy bank a small distance away from the queue of competitors trying to cross. It became clear we wouldn't be able to leap this small river without bringing on muscle tears or cramp. Instead we waited patiently for what would have been our place in the queue had we not taken our shortcut, then took a form of hop, skip and jump to cross the river. Getting wet was unavoidable.

I joined others in a scene reminiscent of a wildlife film set in deepest Africa, a pile of human wildebeest scrambling up the short sandy other side of the crevasse to emerge onto the rugged terrain. I looked behind me to see competitors approaching what they didn't know was a crevasse, wondering why the line of competitors was temporarily disappearing from view.

The course was, fortunately, relatively straightforward hereafter. But the heat wasn't. What had been a largely hydrated body was, just two to three hours after the start, giving me the signs that I was rapidly becoming dehydrated again: a dry, sandy mouth; a deep, thumping, constant painful headache; a deep feeling of weariness.

Checkpoint 2 appeared and two 1.5 litre bottles of water were handed out. This much water was, as usual, synonymous with a difficult section. Combined with the unrelenting heat of the day the roadbook voiced the need for this extra water: 1.5 miles of "sparse small dunes" seemed to take longer than that distance would suggest, as did the two mile stretch of the *Znaigui Erg* dunes. By now I wearily resigned to the inevitabilities of energy-sapping slowness of pace that was the hallmark of stumbling through sand dunes in debilitating heat with too little water.

Emerging from the dunes onto a winding stony track there was the familiar sight: competitors strung out in various states of forward motion, consciousness and ability to move in a straight line. Some were still strongly marching on, others sat on the ground with their heads in their hands. It was nearing that dark time of each day's stage as the barely bearable heat reached its maximum and competitors, even at this late stage of the whole race, queried the sanity of carrying on.

But now I felt good. Now I was out of the dunes I felt strong again on stony terrain. I was sure the IV drip from Monday had done me the power of good over these last couple of days.

Alas, such is the desert: periods of elation can be swiftly followed by grouchiness or tears or dejection.

I came to Checkpoint 3: less than 6.5 miles to go. I took on some food and swigged water from the bottle given to me. A French competitor pulled alongside me and similarly took on food and water. She had a picture of someone pinned to the front of her chest. I assumed she was running for him. She looked in an awful state. I asked if she was okay and she began crying, babbling in between uncontrollable tears.

Blimey, I thought, *she's having a tough time*. She started trotting on. I followed shortly behind her and gradually overtook her. She was suffering… a lot. I raised out my arm and hand and touched her shoulder as I passed in a gesture of encouragement. She cried even more.

Soon though it would be my turn as my own physical state went from feeling okay to feeling wretched again. I took on some sweets and sought out my iPod. In the glaring sun I couldn't see the small screen properly and randomly tapped on the screen until something audible resembling music came through my headphones. I can't for the life of me remember what the music was but, coupled with the relentless heat and feeling utterly exhausted, I started crying too. I wondered if I should wait for the bawling French woman to catch up so we could cross the Stage 5 finish line in Anglo-French mutual miserableness.

On I went. My iPod moved on to something more upbeat and I stopped crying and felt a surge of renewal. I started to run, feeling fantastic again. I passed a British competitor, with whom I'd been swapping race places throughout the day: I don't think I ever saw her not running.

"Keep on plodding on!" she shouted. I picked up what felt like a faster run, feeling strong. Inexplicably I started crying again.

The music had changed once more. Somehow I'd tapped away on my iPod so it was only playing the first couple of minutes of a track before randomly choosing another. This seemed to be affecting my mood.

Sod this, I thought. I switched off my iPod and played uplifting music in my head instead. With the sugar from my sweets infusion now taking effect I once more felt fantastic again.

The track gradually descended through the ruins of the M'Fiss mines and village and I felt strong enough to start running again, a few weathered old Moroccans cheering and clapping me past as they sat on a wall smoking.

In the distance, a couple of miles away at the end of a long stony track, the finish bivouac came into view. Too exhausted to keep running I interspersed a fast march with a jog to eat up the distance. To my left in the further distance I could see tomorrow's challenge: the *Erg Chebbi* dunes, the largest sand dunes in Morocco.

Oh… my… God… I thought, *they are huge!*

I looked away to concentrate on finishing today's task. Running over a long flat stretch to the finish line I felt great once again, powering along in this last stretch to overtake a good couple of dozen of competitors and finally hear that reassuring bleep as I reached the finish mat. As soon as I stopped, I felt nauseous.

Delighted that the day's marathon stage was finished I collected my water and shuffled stiffly towards Tent 78, taking in the awesome beauty but apparently impenetrable huge dunes ahead of me. Even during this relatively short walk the sunlight was changing rapidly enough to present differing shades of oranges and pinks on the distant spectacle.

★★★

The air was pleasantly cooler now. The position of our tent faced out away from the *Erg Chebbi* dunes to deliver us a great view across the flat stony plain to the long run-in of the marathon stage. A couple of mini-races were in progress: we cheered from a distance as some finishers opened up the throttle to pull in a couple of others before the finish line. Every now and then the great view would be interrupted by some competitors undertaking a full strip wash, paying too much detail to cleanliness and too close for comfort.

We shouted disapproval at a Frenchman giving us too much visual information in his detailed attention to washing his naked buttocks.

★ ★ ★

Spirits were high. A short "fun run" tomorrow across the dunes and we'd have completed the Marathon des Sables.

Darkness was falling. I was still patching myself up over dinner as the Paris Symphony Orchestra, flown in every year to give a concert at the end of the penultimate stage, could be heard tuning up.

This was something I didn't want to miss so hurried myself before painfully hobbling over to the horseshoe of people sat in the sand enjoying the concert. The numbers were swelled by some competitors' friends and family who had joined us through the event organisers to experience a sample night in the Sahara desert… in their own bivouac strictly separated from the competitors. My wife, Mum- and Dad-in-law were now in Morocco, having booked a finish line trip with Complete Morocco: I couldn't wait to see them tomorrow.

The symphony orchestra was a delight. I sat awhile taking in the atmosphere: a soprano opera singer singing with gusto in the middle of the Sahara beneath a crystal clear, star-lit sky. It was a pretty impressive experience.

The concert at an end, and now quite cold and stiff having sat a good hour on a stony cold desert floor, I made my way back to Tent 78.

This would be my last night camped out in this amazing place. I wanted to have a good last day and sought to ensure sleep was aided by taking a sleeping tablet.

★ ★ ★

GARMIN FORERUNNER 310XT STATISTICS FOR STAGE 5

Distance: 26.22 miles
Time: 7 hours, 5 minutes, 54 seconds
Elevation gain: 1002 feet
Calories burnt: 2141
Heart Rate Average: 121 beats per minute
Heart Rate Maximum: 165 beats per minute

OFFICIAL RACE STATISTICS

Stage 5 finish position: 533 of 801 starters
Finish time: 7 hours, 2 minutes, 14 seconds
Stage 5 abandonments: 5

11

Stage 6: Merdani to Merzouga: 15.5 km/9.6 miles

> *The brick walls are there for a reason. The brick walls are not there to keep us out. The brick walls are there to give us a chance to show how badly we want something. Because the brick walls are there to stop the people who don't want it badly enough. They're there to stop the other people.*
>
> Randy Pausch, The Last Lecture

Saturday 14 April 2012

The final day. The final stage.

There was a mixture of emotions as final preparations were made before we ambled towards the start line: sadness at the coming end of a unique experience; relief that the hot grind would soon be over; excitement at the prospect of cool, cleansing showers this evening in a 5-star hotel with real food and drink.

But all that had to wait. Although the day's final stage was barely 10 miles it would take us through the *Erg Chebbi* dunes, the largest of all in Morocco. Reaching a height of 150 metres they covered a relatively short area, 6.5 miles at their widest from east to west (and our roadbook showed we would be crossing at about this point), 14 miles north to south. Enough to get lost, though that shouldn't happen for a human snake of several hundred runners.

Having eaten my final batch of cold cereal with rehydrated

milk and quaffed what were by now sickening gulps of electrolyte-induced water I could marvel at the lightness of my rucksack. It couldn't now have weighed much more than four to five kilos. Having almost halved in weight I looked back and wondered at the physical demand of starting out with the energy-sapping weight at the beginning of this race a week ago. Again I found myself having to tighten up the straps on my rucksack; I barely noticed it on my back now. I'd also been losing weight off my body rapidly over the last few days: my shorts felt looser. I hadn't seen myself in a mirror for a week, nor shaved, showered or brushed my teeth (mint chewing gum taking some minor care of dental hygiene with a smaller risk of sickness): I wondered how I looked and how much weight had actually been lost. I certainly felt different.

The start line resembled a carnival atmosphere. Some danced to the strains of the Euro-pop music blasting from the speakers: I use the term "danced" loosely. There was the surreal scene of hundreds of filthy, stinking competitors, adorned with rucksacks, gyrating stiff hips like geriatrics in tight lycra shorts and running tights to modern, Euro-pop, sultry Barry White-type lyrics... *I believe in lurve, ooooh yeah! I'm a crazy dancer...*

It had to be seen to be believed.

Cheers, smiles and hugs were all around. It felt an odd sensation: a jubilant air with a sadness at its core.

All of us from Tent 78 shook hands, hugged, slapped backs: *See you at the hotel!* For the last time our musical friend that saw us off for every stage of the race, AC/DC's *Highway to Hell*, boomed from the speakers... *Five... Four... Three... Two... One...* roars of cheering.

We poured over the start line. Some were crying but all were ecstatic, even if the majority could barely walk or run properly. The media helicopter roared above us to whoops and hollers before it soon flew back over us in its sideways acrobatics, inducing the involuntary huge grin and cheers.

Then the near-silence descended for the last time with the odd tinge of competitors' chatter and the hundreds of pairs of legs shuffling across the stony plateau.

The roadbook showed us the way: a near straight line for four miles to Checkpoint 1 across a near flat stony plain. No water would be distributed at Checkpoint 1: an extra bottle had been distributed to us this morning along with the standard issue 1.5 litre bottle. Most of this I'd already drunk in an effort to rehydrate for what I hoped would be a final hard push.

It was easy to follow the carnival procession to Checkpoint 1. Most of it was easily runnable, a surprising feat after the 144 miles that were already in our legs from the last several days.

Conversation and chit-chat was few and far between: we were all on a mission now to make this a quick finish. Checkpoint 1 arrived and soon passed as a 234 degree turn towards the east took us directly into the scorching dunes, the final sting in the tail.

The dunes started gently but rapidly became beasts. Fortunately we weren't being taken over the few truly massive dunes: they looked impossible to ascend. Unfortunately those plentiful younger brother dunes remained imposing.

And so the almost six mile sand slog began. I'd felt great thus far along with everyone else but soon a reasonable pace across a stony plateau became a slow, weary trudge. The upside was that we wouldn't have to endure this today for hour upon hour of unbearable heat.

It was time to admire the scenery. Goals of a fast finish diminished. Instead I wanted to enjoy every last minute, to absorb this other-worldly scene.

These dunes were indeed tough: steep, steep ascents with steep, steep declines down the other side of their peak. Some did require a hands and knees approach to getting over them, either by choice because of the effort required or by having fallen, exhausted, into the deep sand.

And literally nothing at all but sand: not a stone, not a rock, no camel grass. Nothing but various beautiful hues of deep, roasting sand. The light subtly changed as I moved slowly across, playing out different shades and textures. It was a wonderful natural phenomenon to see.

I'd noticed that some competitors were making their way across the ridge lines of the dunes: this was taking a longer time and increasing the distance covered as that course meandered away from and back again to the direct compass bearing to the finish. I'd initially followed everyone else ahead of me but what had been a hard crust of sand for the leading competitors was by now for the mid-packers a mush of sinking sand: it wasn't fun to constantly descend up to mid-calves and use spent quad muscles to pull the legs back out, or sink backwards after the effort of having moved forward just a few steps.

Looking ahead of me I saw that a more direct line, following as closely as possible the compass bearing given, showed far fewer footprints. But taking this slight change of course would mean enduring the full impact of the dunes' steepness on exhausted legs.

I took a deep hot breath and plumped for the more direct line over the next couple of dunes: I found myself gaining on competitors ahead of me. Surprisingly my quad muscles now felt strong: tired, yes, but still with sufficient strength and energy to allow me to power my legs up the dunes.

Before long this was becoming extremely wearing, but I was still gaining on others. Behind me a few other competitors had taken a similar view: the game of cat and mouse was on. This together with the knowledge of a finish getting ever closer gave little boosts of adrenalin. I started to eat a few of my final day's supply of jelly beans.

A few people ahead of me had stopped to admire some ramshackle "buildings" seemingly dropped in the middle of this dune field. We'd seen nothing but sand for miles. I caught up too and took a quick photo of this oddity: we were still a good four miles from the village of Merzouga yet here in the middle of nowhere appeared to be someone's home. Old threadbare heavy cotton sheets provided the canvas, slung over thick supporting sticks driven into the sand. I looked around for any sign of life other than the several hundred competitors around me.

Way above me to my right I spotted a lone figure sat cross-legged atop a steep, tall orange-yellow sand dune. His dark, sand- and wind-battered face was just visible from the spotlessly clean white headcloth keeping his head protected. He seemed to be dressed in cotton robes similar to those forming what I presumed was his Berber home that I was now stood alongside. He was simply admiring the view, wondering quizzically no doubt at this gaggle of madmen and women snaking perhaps pointlessly to Merzouga. *How peaceful*, I thought. Framed behind and above him was a bright blue sky that climbed through gradations to a darker blue. I stole a quick photo, the imagery of solitude already burned in my mind, and trudged on ahead, the Berber's line of vision pointing me to the snaking line to the finish and, eventually, the decadent ease and plenty of home.

Eventually I began to sense an imminent finish. I could hear a helicopter in the distance. Before us though was an unavoidable steep climb: we were at the base of a sandy bowl and ahead appeared to be the ridge beyond which I hoped I would see the finish.

I pushed deep. Step by step I worked my way to the top of the ridge, sinking along the way, trying to drive forward and up. Finally I reached this peak, exhausted. The hotter temperatures were coming.

I still had a way to go but I felt a huge sense of relief at the distant sight of activity: a village, a couple of towers, noise.

Beforehand though there were more dunes to cross, albeit now smaller. They descended ahead of me before rising again to a final crest which really would then give me sight of the finish.

I tried to swallow more jelly beans for the final slog but found this difficult as I was by now too dehydrated to eat properly. We were all speeding up now, touching the limits of our fitness in this final push.

I descended a last steep dune and instantly knew the *Erg Chebbi* dunes were over: I was descending across stones and rocks. I crossed this stony base to rise up a last sandy ascent… *and there it was! The finish!*

Barely half a mile now. Friends and families of competitors were here having ventured across the sands to this point to cheer us on. They looked as jubilant as we did. A huge smile came across my face. The end was visible in every way: the buses which would take us back to our hotel, the finish gantry with its signage, lines of locals, tourists, friends, family, race volunteers, lining the spectator barriers in the last chute to the finish.

I ran, I sprinted… as best I could. I felt elated, jubilant, complete: I couldn't help from smiling, adrenalin was coursing through me now.

I powered over the last few metres. I forced down the final feeling of nausea.

Bleep… The audible signal that my GPS transponder had now registered my race was at an end, 246.5 km or 153 miles and seven days from the start. No pain, no sickness. Just utter relief and joy that it was all finished and a tremendous amount of satisfaction at having completed "the toughest footrace on earth".

I couldn't help from smiling like a maniac. I joined a queue lining up in front of Patrick Bauer to receive a finisher's medal. Over to my right I was delighted to see my Dad-in-law waving and taking a picture and, further along, my wife and Mum-in-law. It was great to see them: a connection with home.

"*Bonjour* Patrick!"

"*Bonjour* Mark! Well done! Congratulations!"

Patrick Bauer, the creator of this incredible gathering of

humanity, placed my finisher's medal over my stiff neck. Both of us laughing, we grabbed each other in the traditional massive bear hug. I told him what a fantastic event this was and then moved on, newly minted with my Marathon des Sables Finisher's medal.

I went over to the spectator barrier and grabbed my wife for a huge hug: apparently I didn't smell that bad. She was tearful, I was tearful.

I moved on to collect my lunch bag and numbered bus ticket: I had 45 minutes before I needed to join my bus back to the Berber Palace hotel. First I desperately needed to sit down.

Having met up with my family we took shelter from the heat in a Moroccan canvas tent. My wife took a head-shot photo of me: unshaven for a week, visibly having lost weight, my face slightly burnt and caked in dirt and sand, my once-clean cotton top now filthy, my plastic bottles sat in Raidlight bottle holders a breeding ground of germs, the red ribbon around my neck indicating the medal that said it was all worth it. I beam in that photo: peaceful, relaxed.

I ate a little: I didn't yet have my appetite back nor much ability to move my mouth properly. Around us shattered-looking competitors sat reflecting on the end.

It was too soon, it felt, but it was time to board my bus. I looked around, desperately trying to absorb into my being the smells, the colours, the people, the views of the competitors still coming over the finish line to their own ecstatic finish. My wife, Dad- and Mum-in-law went to join up with the Complete Morocco organisers for their journey back to the Berber Palace hotel.

And then it started to hit me as I wandered to find my bus. Jubilance now tinged with sadness.

The bus was almost full when I got on; it wasn't long before we would leave. I ate some more and sipped plenty. It felt alien to be sitting on a chair, odd to see so much activity around me.

The bus pulled away to begin the long six hour journey back

to Ouarzazate. While wallowing in a jubilant feeling of having completed something I would never forget I continued to desperately soak up the desert scenery around me… and reflect.

Back in the mid-1990s, when I'd first started running, cycling and swimming in my mid-20s, when I felt I'd conquered the world by having run non-stop for an hour for the first time in my life, the Marathon des Sables was an extreme oddity I had read about in running magazines and national newspapers, a distant something that I would never do. I remember thinking even back then: *that's just too far, too much, too crazy*. There was no way on Earth I was going to be completing that: it was beyond my limits of comprehension.

But now I too had completed what had begun as the original toughest footrace on Earth. I'd decided to do it in what some might see as my own mid-life crisis: back in 2009 I'd seen an overweight, over-tired desk-jockey with no balance other than towards work. It didn't feel good.

Almost three years previously I'd started this journey. In the summer of 2009 while on holiday I'd come back from a hot 20 minute run, my first in a long, long time, out of breath, sweating profusely and wondering where all that fitness and more positive view of life from being active outside of work had all gone. Less than three years later I was sat on a bus in the Sahara desert, a Marathon des Sables Finisher's medal around my neck after 153 miles in seven days crossing beautifully inspiring empty landscapes through brutal heat.

I had needed to do something after four years of inactivity, to run from the encroaching shadows of adult-onset diabetes and other modern ailments that would surely arrive from being overweight, over-tired and doing little else but work, go home, eat then sleep.

After several hours, as the bus neared the heights of spoilt living (hot food, luxurious cotton sheets, freely available cold drinks, running water to drink and shower in...), I resolved I was never going to go back to old ways and habits.

The Marathon des Sables had seemed the best way to emerge from those shadows. And I'd finally done it.

★ ★ ★

GARMIN FORERUNNER 310XT STATISTICS FOR STAGE 6

Distance: 9.31 miles
Time: 2 hours, 44 minutes, 35 seconds
Elevation gain: 676 feet
Calories burnt: 1118
Heart Rate Average: 127 beats per minute
Heart Rate Maximum: 164 beats per minute

OFFICIAL RACE STATISTICS

Stage 6 finish position: 484 of 796 starters
Finish time: 2 hours, 44 minutes, 40 seconds
Stage 6 abandonments: 2

Overall General Classification: 550 of 853 starters; total time 51 hours, 16 minutes, 56 seconds
(including 2 hour time penalty for IV drip)

12

Emerging from Shadows

May 2013

I look back to an extraordinary event and a genuinely life-changing experience: so many sights, sounds, feelings and memories are indelibly etched onto my mind.

Once back at the hotel it took an hour and three showers to get clean again. Finally able to look in a mirror I saw a significantly slimmer me.

It wasn't long after returning to the hotel that Tent 78 congregated in the restaurant for a feast to end all feasts: most of us devoured three full platefuls of buffet food for dinner (after having had a lunch with my family of a pizza or two each) and, the following morning, three full platefuls for breakfast. Once home I found I was still lighter than when I'd left: I had lost the best part of a stone in weight, between six and seven kilos, in a week.

We all agreed that what experiencing the Marathon des Sables brought into sharp focus, aside from the understanding that sand is very difficult to cross on foot, was what is most valuable in life: the simple things and family. We all missed wives and children, we all had visions of what we would do once back home, working lives would become of less consequence, resolutions were made.

A strange thought, perhaps, for any person who hasn't endured very basic living in extreme temperatures in the world's hottest desert for 153 miles of hard physical and mental effort coupled with severe sleep-deprivation over seven days carrying a heavy rucksack with a restricted water supply. But a very obvious and easily understood awareness for anyone who has. The temporary deprivations at the time felt very much more permanent during the toughest hours of the event and gave rise to a resolve to never again fail to fully appreciate everything we had.

Would I go back? At the time I was very clear: "*Never again!*" But barely a couple of days later, as injuries gradually began to heal, as life became more comfortable once again, those thoughts became "*Well, actually, I* could *do it again…* "

As time passed the painful memories faded. I know now that at the end of Stage 2 I must have been in a very poor state, fallen to the ground surrounded by small pools of my own vomit; I know too I must have felt in some pain, that I felt a pronounced sense of utter exhaustion like none experienced before. But I am also now aware that my mind helpfully plays the trick that this is mere *knowledge* of certain feelings and events that happened in the past: I have no present actual experience of them.

Soon after the race I wasn't sure about going back for a second attempt. Why go back to do something extreme I'd already completed once? But I soon came to understand why a few do go back to the Moroccan Sahara, and also why, for many Marathon des Sables veterans, some go on to continue feeding an addiction to removing the detritus of modern day life from one's mind at other extreme endurance events: to satisfy the craving for a sheer intensity of experience, a heightened sense of awareness and presence, despite the traumas that can occur.

Whenever I think back to the joyous moments of the race I feel physical effects, a small adrenaline surge, more mental positivity, a great feeling that makes me smile: seeing the small Moroccan girl beaming at the gifts of Canadian maple-leaf badges and shouting out "Canada!"; pouring a bucket of cold water over each other after Stage 1 as Mark and I found a desert well just outside the bivouac; opening and drinking an ice-cold can of Coke; the weird feel-good sensations after almost 40 miles on Stage 4 that saw me flying across the sand a singing, hyper, sugar-induced hallucinating madman; the unadulterated feeling of exuberance at crossing the finish line.

Such is the marvel of human biology that allows humans to repeat feats that rational thought should prevent. So, yes, I would go back to try and complete the Marathon des Sables a second time, and possibly a third, and a fourth... Like a shot.

I'd been aware before I left for Morocco of other finishers' stories of coming back to a post-Marathon des Sables blues, a bump back down to Earth. Something that had taken up a significant portion of my life was now gone. I understood the comments of MdS-veterans, a club of which I was now a member, of feelings of there being a hole or a void in one's life.

Training for and completing the event, and the combination of gruelling and life-enriching experiences I had during the race, had made me realise a number of things: I'd reconnected with the enjoyment I used to have for training and keeping fit as a mid- to back-of the field runner, the alternative focus it gives away from work. It made me realise on a far wider level that it was perfectly possible to look at the seemingly impossible or unlikely and consider the catalyst for greater things: taking that first step.

As a result I committed to change. First of all I decided to commit myself to ensuring that keeping fit and strong and completing events remained a continuing focus: I didn't want to go back to those feelings of sluggishness and constant tiredness associated with being overweight and overworked.

It didn't go entirely to plan at first. Soon after getting home, having resolved as my next long-term goal the completion of 100 marathons and ultra-marathons (83 to go, at the time), I ran the Baslow Boot Bash barely two months after the Marathon des Sables. An off-road marathon distance event around the Derbyshire hills near Chatsworth it was clear by mile 11 I was in for a tough time: my legs were nowhere near recovered. Too many stiles and a quick run away from an annoyed bull in a field brought on the most painful of cramps in my legs. I finished what ended up being a hilly 28 mile event in a sorry state, running and walking from side-to-side like a Weeble.

I was also at this time ignoring a chest infection which I seemed to have picked up either during or shortly after the Marathon des Sables, not helped I'm sure by lungs scoured by sand. By the end of August 2012, with another two marathons ticked off, I was still worn out.

I decided to listen to my body and took time out for a period of recovery.

By January 2013 some of the weight I had lost had climbed back on. Where was I to go now? Was I losing the impetus of change that I'd brought back from Morocco? I had the desire to want to change things permanently but not quite yet the tools to do so: with my goal in my head of completing 100 marathons and ultra-marathons, along with the seedling of ambition to join the 4 Deserts Club (a club with, at the time of writing, 125 members from across the world including only 17 Brits), I figured that one person who would know where I was and where I could go was the guy who'd made the point during an ITV documentary about the 2008 Marathon des Sables that the race changes people.

So I went to see Rory Coleman, a performance coach, marathon and ultra-marathon runner with (at the time) 9 Marathon des Sables completions, over 750 completed marathons and 9 Guinness World Records. Rory looked a good five to ten years younger than his 50 with a level of fitness that would put most of Britain's people in their 20s to shame.

On a cold winter's day in early January I met Rory in his local gym in Cardiff and explained where my mind was in what I wanted to do. I'd already by now, in a post-Marathon des Sables change to my outlook on life, decided to abandon my profession as a lawyer and pursue a more gratifying occupation based on doing what I enjoyed in an area that had fascinated me since my teenage years (Post-MdS Resolution number 1: do what interests me).

An hour later I was collapsed on the gym floor panting for life and sweating buckets, my muscles screaming from lactic acid. After a short introduction to Rory's Powerhour and a punishing weights session it was clear any fitness I'd had at the end of last August after my last marathon was almost gone. After delighting in taking a picture of me collapsed on the floor, we went for a chat back at Rory's home.

With skill he carefully built up the mental acceptance of being able to do just about anything, if only I'd leave my mind open.

"Have you any idea how many Brits have completed the MdS?" he asked. "A couple of thousand, tops? You're one of them. On a scale from here to here, you're there, almost at the end of the scale." Rory drew with his finger across the mirror a long line, finally pointing towards almost the end of it.

"So what do you want to do next? Another one? Something else?"

Rory carefully took notes. We then got onto the discussion about food and weight, and losing more of it.

"You're addicted."

"Really? To what?" I asked.

"Sugar. Crap food. Diet Coke."

He may have had a point. Although I'd significantly reduced my intake I hadn't really kicked it enough to make a real difference.

Rory then set about explaining that, if I were to follow his 12 week plan, there were certain things I could no longer eat and other things I could no longer do if I were serious about my athletic goals.

"But... " I spluttered, "how would I cope for lunch?!?"

Rory looked at me, slightly nodding his head towards my slight paunch: "Dunno... But... " patting his stomach now with the flat of his hand, "... you've already eaten it."

A couple of hours later I was driving home fired with enthusiasm, thinking ahead.

I would, one day, run the Marathon des Sables again. Yes, I would complete at least 100 marathons and ultra-marathons. I would sign up and attempt to finish Racing the Planet's 4 Desert Series, ultra-marathons across the coldest, the hottest, the windiest and the driest deserts in the world.

Once home I checked my email. Rory had already sent me my 12 week training and food plan, to begin in just two days. I gulped at the enormity of it all.

It wasn't easy. It was hard work.

But after those 12 weeks I had lost almost 1.5 stone in weight and completed another two marathons with a strength I'd never had before. I was by now completing two marathons a month, one of them being my fastest in 11 years. I began to wonder how much better I could have performed in my Marathon des Sables.

I was finally emerging from those shadows on a more permanent basis.

I signed up to race the next edition of Racing the Planet's 156 mile 4 Desert Series Sahara Race, and a new journey began.

13
Epilogue

October 2013

The author has, since the MdS 2012, worked with performance coach Rory Coleman to reach a standard of fitness not seen since his late-20s. This has resulted in some of his fastest marathon times achieved during 2013. With 38 marathons and ultra-marathons completed, including 33 races, the author aims to complete the 4 Deserts Series encompassing multi-day ultra-races across the hottest, driest, windiest and coldest deserts on Earth: the Sahara Race, the Atacama Crossing, the Gobi March and The Last Desert (Antarctica). Unless the MdS distracts him along the way… In the meantime the author continues to work towards completing 100 marathons and ultra-marathons.

Mark achieved a 3 hour 45 minute marathon in the months after his MdS 2012. Plagued with injuries to his ankle over many years he had an operation in the summer of 2013 to try and resolve it but still manages regular runs of up to 13 miles and is now building back up to run longer distances. Mark became more focussed on cycling during his injury period, joining a cycling club and racking up completions of various sportives and mountain bike races. An Ironman-distance triathlon has emerged as a new challenge to aim for.

Ash was out of running action for much of 2013 having put his foot in a hole while running down a Welsh mountain, tearing ligaments and tendons in the process. While hoping to start running again soon he's keen to return to the MdS feeling as though he didn't do as well as he could have in the 2012 race (finishing 266th of 853 starters). Ash is now looking at completing three 100 mile non-stop ultra-marathons in order to qualify for the Badwater Ultramarathon: 135 miles non-stop through California's Death Valley.

Paul, a self-proclaimed non-runner despite a good turn of speed whose catchphrase after the MdS became "I would never do the MdS again, you understand, but if I did, which I definitely won't be, I would do the following differently... ", confessed "although I feel like a bit of a fraud, I have decided to have a go at the MdS again in 2015 (provided I can get an entry)... " Paul has also confessed to taking a sneaky look at the Badwater Ultramarathon.

Wayne also caught the ultra-running bug after experiencing his own post-MdS revelations. Wayne is in training for the January 2014 edition of The Spine Challenger, a 108-mile non-stop winter mountain marathon across the Pennine Way between Edale and Hawes... with a 60-hour time limit... with 4890 metres of ascent. After this he plans on completing the Great Lakeland 3Day and the dreaded Dragon's Back Race ("One of the World's toughest mountain running races"). Wayne's also found the time to set up a triathlon club and joined with some friends to launch a website with highly entertaining blogs dedicated to ultra-running (http://ultramadness.co.uk).

Richard continues to rack up his tally of half- and full marathons. Over time he has become increasingly tempted by a second stab at the MdS having initially said "Never again"... as long as his son also wants to do it.

Dean continued and ratcheted up a punishing training regime to become one of only eleven people in the world to have reached the finish line of the non-stop 350-mile 6633 Extreme Winter Ultra Marathon, one of only four finishers of the 2013 edition of the race.

Appendix 1

Marathon des Sables 2012
Weights in Grammes and Kit List

Compulsory Equipment	
Signal mirror	16
Anti-venom pump (with duct tape)	35
Aluminium survival blanket	78
Rucksack	677
Sleeping bag (including 12g bag)	567
Head torch with batteries	87
Spare batteries	35
10 safety pins	3
Compass	20
Lighter	15
Whistle (on rucksack)	0
Swiss card with knife/scissors	22
Topical disinfectant (25ml iodine in Medical Kit)	35
Lakeland ziplock bag	7
€200	10
Compulsory Equipment Total	*1607*

Other Equipment	
Passport	36
Plastic wallet including credit/debit cards	25
Waist pouch	141
Toilet roll pack x 7 (including gloves)	161
Esbit titanium stove	13

Esbit titanium spork	16
Esbit solid fuel tabs x 1 pack (20 tabs)	80
Esbit titanium cooking pot	114
High5 Zero Berry Sports tabs x 20	85
High5 Zero Cherry Orange Sports tabs x 20	97
Elete Electrolyte 25ml x 2	73
Raidlight bottle holders x 2	76
Camelbak Podium 710ml bottle x 2 (with Performance bottle top)	216
Adidas Evil Eye bag, headband & clear lenses	46
Adidas Flip flops	289
Orbit Complete Spearmint gum x 14	35
Other Equipment Total	*1503*

Medical Kit

Ciprofloxacin x 10	13
Large safety pin	0
Lip balm	10
Immodium Instants x 12	2
Paracetamol 500mg x 16	12
25ml iodine (see Compulsory Equipment: Topical disinfectant)	0
Lakeland ziplock bag	7
Buccastem x 8	2
Leukotape	18
Wemmi wipes x 6	23
Cuticura hygiene gel 100ml	110
BodyGlide	33
P20 approx. 70ml	77
Boots micropur tablets x 14	1
Boots Sleepeaze tabs x 4	1
Boots silicone earplugs x 4	22
Anti-histamine	5

NipGuards x 6 pairs	3
Medical Kit Total	*339*

Luxuries

Thermarest sleeping mat	206
Spare pair Thorlos mini crew socks	71
Spare pair shorts	120
Icebreaker GT 150 Ultralite merino wool T-shirt	150
PowerMonkey solar panels	78
PowerMonkey battery	81
Garmin Forerunner 310XT watch	77
Garmin charging clip with USB tip	46
iPod Nano 16GB with guard	23
Sony headphones	27
PowerMonkey iPod connector	5
Pad, pencil and sharpener	51
Disposable camera	96
British flag	30
Luxuries Total	*1061*

Gross Total (excluding Food)	4,510
Total Weight of Food	4,159
Rucksack Weight Before Race Items:	8,669
Weight of water (2x710ml)	1420
Estmated flare weight	350
Estimated roadbook weight	100
Estimated weight: 8 toilet sachets	75
Estimated salt tablets weight	75

TOTAL RUCKSACK WEIGHT	10,689

Appendix 2

Marathon des Sables 2012
Food and Calories

Stage 1: 2553 calories

Tesco Crunchy Oats with coconut, sultana & almond 138g	621
Tesco Instant Dried Skimmed Milk 50g	182
Original Peperami 25g	126
Tesco jumbo roasted salted peanuts 25g	145
Nature Valley Canadian Maple Syrup Crunchy Bar 42g	191
Tesco Jelly Beans 25g	95
ForGoodnessShakes Superberry 72g	260
Mountain House Spaghetti Bolognaise 142g	716
High5 Energy Bar Coconut 60g	217
Stage 1 food pack weight in grammes:	*640*
Stage 1 food pack total calories:	*2553*

Stage 2: 2614 calories

Jordans Crunchy Oat Granola Tropical Fruits 143g	620
Tesco Instant Dried Skimmed Milk 50g	182
Original Peperami 25g	126
Tesco jumbo roasted salted peanuts 50g	290
High5 Energy Bar Coconut 60g	217
ForGoodnessShakes Vanilla 72g	261
ExtremeAdventure Curried Beef with Rice 174g	800
Nature Valley Fruit & Nut Bar 42g	118

Stage 2 food pack weight in grammes:	*652*
Stage 2 food pack total calories:	*2614*

Stage 3: 2904 calories

Expedition Foods Fruity Muesli with Milk Powder 180g	813
Original Peperami 25g	126
Tesco jumbo roasted salted peanuts 25g	145
Tesco jelly beans 50g	185
Nature Valley Fruit & Nut Bar 42g	118
ForGoodnessShakes Superberry 72g	260
Mountain House Chilli Con Carne with Rice 200g	1066
Nature Valley Canadian Maple Syrup Crunchy Bar 42g	191
Stage 3 food pack weight in grammes:	*683*
Stage 3 food pack total calories:	*2904*

Stage 4, day 1: 3164 calories

Tesco Crunchy Oats with coconut, sultana & almond 138g	621
Tesco Instant Dried Skimmed Milk 50g	182
Tesco jumbo roasted salted peanuts 100g	570
High5 Energy Bar Coconut 60g	217
Rowntree's Sour Faces 50g	162
M&S Peppered Beef Jerky 50g	160
Jordans Crunchy Oat Granola Tropical Fruits 143g	620
Tesco Instant Dried Skimmed Milk 50g	182
Rowntree's Sour Faces 100g	324
Original Peperami 25g	126
Stage 4, day 1 food pack weight in grammes	*832*
Stage 4, day 1 food pack total calories:	*3164*

Stage 4, day 2: 2195 calories

Expedition Foods Porridge with Sultanas 160g	806
Nature Valley Fruit & Nut Bar 42g	118
Original Peperami 25g	126
M&S Peppered Beef Jerky 50g	160
Nature Valley Canadian Maple Syrup Crunchy Bar 42g	191
Mountain House Chilli Con Carne With Rice 100g	533
ForGoodnessShakes Vanilla 72g	261
Stage 4, day 2 food pack weight in grammes:	*471*
Stage 4, day 2 food pack total calories:	*2195*

Stage 5: 2441 calories

Jordans Crunchy Oat Granola Tropical Fruits 143g	620
Tesco Instant Dried Skimmed Milk 50g	182
Original Peperami 25g	126
M&S Peppered Beef Jerky 50g	160
Tesco jelly beans 50g	185
Nature Valley Canadian Maple Syrup Crunchy Bar 42g	191
ForGoodnessShakes Vanilla 72g	261
Mountain House Spaghetti Bolognaise 142g	716
Stage 5 food pack weight in grammes:	*638*
Stage 5 food pack total calories:	*2441*

Stage 6: 869 calories

Tesco Crunchy Oats with coconut, sultana & almond 90g	390
Tesco Instant Dried Skimmed Milk 30g	109
Tesco Jelly Beans 100g	370
Stage 6 food pack weight in grammes:	*243*
Stage 6 food pack total calories:	*869*

Total food packs weight in grammes: Stages 1-6	*4159*
Total food packs calories: Stages 1-6	*16740*

Appendix 3

Kit Choices and Comment

These kit choices and comments are solely those of the author: any potential competitor in the Marathon des Sables must reach his or her own views on what to choose and what works. Kit choices, technologies and race methods change over time and experience: the author may use different items of kit and methods on future similar such events. The author has not been paid or sponsored by any individual or organisation referred to in this Appendix or anywhere else in this book.

I wouldn't need to carry much during my MdS but what I did carry would need to be robust and as light a weight as possible.

A lot of time was saved by taking a look at outdoor-gear store Likeys and its Desert Kit List along with hours spent on reviewing numerous websites, blogs and bulletin boards checking out what previous competitors thought. Over time I finally reached my own kit list for the event the details of which are shown in Appendix 1.

Below are some general notes on decisions made for certain items of kit with a post-race comment added based on my experiences during the event.

Shoes

I'd finally found my road shoe of choice after years going through all sorts of poorly performing shoes, the Asics Gel Nimbus, and had had many comfortable runs on the road, the treadmill and compacted summer trails. I needed a neutral gait shoe as my orthotics would solve my mild overpronation and the Nimbus did the job. My off road shoe of choice was the neutral gait Asics Gel Trabuco.

The question was: which type of shoe for the desert?

Any kind of Gore-Tex lined shoe was out of the question: I didn't want trench foot after the first day of the event. I did though want as much cushioning as I could get and as comfortable a journey as possible, so the road shoe became my choice for the MdS. Yes, I wouldn't come across roads in the desert but, with gaiters sewn on to my shoes and much of the terrain being compacted sand and stones or rocks, my road shoe would do the job.

Finally, what size? As the feet swell in hot conditions my standard size 10s (extra width) would be very uncomfortable after a day in the desert. Some comments I found referred to the need to have a shoe that was two sizes bigger than normal but that sounded ridiculous to me.

I settled for one size bigger than normal, in extra width shoes to accommodate my wide foot. My dual sock combination would fill out any space in the shoe until the inevitable swelling from the heat took up any room.

Dependent on how bad the swelling would become I then had a number of options to adopt my feet to the size of shoe: remove one of my two pairs of socks, loosen the laces sufficiently, or remove an orthotic (as a last resort).

Post-race comment: the road shoe worked very well. Very little sand got in to my shoes thanks to the Sandbaggers gaiters (see below) and other than a pre-event heel blister that got significantly worse I experienced just a few small end-of-toe blisters. After Stage 4 I no longer wore the Injinji sock on my left foot to accommodate for that. One size bigger than normal for my shoe was plenty: it took a few hours on Stage 1 for my feet to swell to accommodate the extra room but thereafter I never felt my shoes to be too tight or loose.

Socks

At an early stage of my longer distance training runs I was suffering instep blisters. I quickly resolved this by wearing Injinji "toe socks", fitting the foot and its toes as a glove does for the hand and its fingers. With a pair of cushioned Thorlos running socks this combination was very comfortable and would be my choice with my extra-width running shoes that were one size bigger than normal.

For a psychological boost I took one extra pair of the Thorlos socks for a change half way through the event.

Post-race comment: I shook out whatever sand had got through to my feet at the end of each stage but this sock combination together with the Sandbaggers gaiters did a great job in keeping my feet relatively healthy and problem-free.

Shorts

Tight fitting running shorts (to eliminate chaffing) or long running tights? I didn't fancy the latter: I already knew my choice of gaiters would come up to my knees and, if I had longs on underneath, my legs would surely boil.

I'd never got on with running shorts that flapped around while running so tight fitting shorts were the norm for me: I'd found the placing of the seams in the Nike Dri-Fit shorts didn't cause chaffing (particularly when using lots of BodyGlide) so this was an easy choice.

Post-race comment: no issues experienced with this combination of applying BodyGlide every morning and wearing these Nike Dri-Fit shorts.

Gaiters

How to keep the sand out of my running shoes to ensure maximum blister prevention?

The knee-length parachute silk gaiters supplied by Sandbaggers were legendary and had great reviews. They wouldn't win anything in the running attire fashion stakes but with a draw cord at the knee to keep them up they sounded the ideal job. It would also mean less sunscreen that I needed to carry to cover my lower legs.

About a month before I flew out to Morocco I sent off to Sandbaggers my size 11 running shoes for a line of velcro to be glued and stitched around the outside of both shoes; the gaiters would then attach to the outside velcro strip.

Post-race comment: these did a fantastic job in keeping the sand out. Many competitors were sporting well-known rival brands but after just a couple of days many were in a very poor state. Inevitably some toe-box scuffing occurred (as you'd expect: these gaiters are, after all, made of parachute silk) but damage was minimised by applying a strip of electrical duct tape at first. However, the desert heat simply melts this type of duct tape. Leukotape was far stronger and did a better repair job for the week, albeit a fresh strip needed to be applied daily at various points on the bottom of the gaiter as the week progressed.

Running top

I wasn't too keen on the idea of a short-sleeved running top because of the risk of sun damage, nor of a stifling tight-fitting top.

I found the ideal solution through Sandbaggers and their supply of Railraiders' Ecomesh shirts: long-sleeved and loose-fitting, the featherweight quick-drying nylon fabric also had a 30+ sunblock protection factor.

Post-race comment: I suffered no sunburn at all in using this top despite not using any sunscreen on areas of my body covered by it. After two days of sweat evaporation and mineral loss in the desert my top resembled a stiff piece of cardboard but it continued to do a good job. No chafing experienced.

Headgear

A baseball cap would be inadequate without neck protection and going without any head protection at all was simply not an option.

I found some desert headgear to be a little light on coverage of the face and neck. The only one I found that was both versatile (to help deal with sandstorms) and could give enough head cover was Frillneck's polyester micromesh hat. I had to get this delivered from Australia in the end but it arrived quickly enough.

I also settled for two Buffs, famous for their versatility: for general wiping of any sweaty brow, to keep my head warm while sleeping in the cold desert air and for covering my face in sandstorms (along with my Frillneck hat).

Post-race comment: the Frillneck was a highly versatile hat and gave excellent coverage for the neck, head and face from the scorching sun. It covered pretty much most of my head in sandstorms, though for a tighter seal against airborne sand I used it in combination with my Buffs.

Watch

I settled for my trusty Garmin Forerunner 310XT to keep track of time, distance and heart rate. But with only a maximum 20 hour battery life I had the issue of how to power it once the battery went flat.

A solar charger was the answer and my research took me to the PowerMonkey Explorer. All I would need was sun!

Post-race comment: my Garmin survived as did my PowerMonkey. By strapping the PowerMonkey solar panel to the top of my rucksack at the beginning of each day and zipping away the attached PowerMonkey battery I managed to get enough charge out on the race stage which, when topped up by leaving it outside for what was left of the post-race evening, kept the Garmin successfully powered.

Rucksack

I'd bought my OMM 32 litre rucksack at an early stage and put it through its paces over many outings: it proved to be almost bomb-proof. The only difficulty I had with it was accessing water bottles from the side mesh pockets, which were too high.

To solve this I adapted the rucksack by using two Raidlight bottle holders and threading through each onto the front straps of the OMM rucksack: in this way, I had easy access to my water bottles without having to remove them. I simply had to turn and lower my head slightly to drink from the bottle.

The only down side to any rucksack is the inability to access much on the move without removing it: side pouches carry little. I had tried the next recommendation of wearing a chest pouch but quickly ditched this idea when trialling it on a long run: with a piece of carrying equipment on both my back and my chest I was overheating on a humid UK summer's day so figured this combination would not work for me in the desert.

My next trial was the solution: a 3 litre OMM waist pouch so I could access everything I'd need on the move from around my waist, freeing my chest to dissipate whatever heat it could.

Post-race comment: the ideal combination. Only rarely did I need to take the rucksack off my back during any stage. Both this rucksack and the waist pouch are still going strong many months and many events later.

Water bottles

My own tests of the Raidlight water bottle showed it to be poorly designed: at 750ml capacity it was ideal but its size meant the bottle when full would swing around on my rucksack straps; the bottle, top and drinking straw combination also meant that any electrolyte tablet added to the water that would give off the smallest of fizz just meant I had a leaking bottle. Even with plain water, it didn't seem to do a great job of keeping the water where it should be: in the bottle.

Eventually I found a different solution: two Camelbak Podium water bottles with the tops swapped for the bottle tops from the Camelbak Performance water bottle.

The former has a twist-top for opening the bottle valve but the bottle would need to be removed from my rucksack and tipped to drink from it; for drinking on the move, the latter was better: a similar twist would open the bottle valve but the built-in straw with a bite valve meant I could drink from the bottle without having to remove the bottle from the Raidlight bottle holders.

Those two bottles would give me access to 1.42 litres of fluid between checkpoints. As each water bottle distributed at each checkpoint measured 1.5 litres I could simply drink the rest or use it to douse my head. I would simply carry any extra bottles distributed.

At the end of each stage it was also easy to simply remove the bite valve and the straw, and drop both into the bottle of water with an added Boots Micropur water purification tablet to do its job overnight.

Post-race comment: hygienically and practically the method worked well. The only possible downside which would need to be tested another time is the effect of direct sun onto clear plastic bottles: after a few hours the water carried a very distinctive plastic taste and smell, which on occasion was nausea-inducing. I wondered if the opaque Raidlight bottles, despite their other downsides, would avoid this.

Spare kit

I opted for just having a spare pair of Thorlos socks to change into after a few days.

A loose pair of shorts would be a pleasant change at the end of each stage to wander and sleep in the bivouac, as would a lightweight short sleeved Icebreaker GT 150 Ultralight merino wool T-shirt.

Finally foot hygiene would be key: I cut off various parts of an airy Adidas sandal to save weight from an otherwise heavy shoe which would allow my feet to breathe and try and recover after each day.

Post-race comment: I don't think I would have missed the spare pair of Thorlos though it did feel good to put on a clean pair of socks part-way through the week. It was very welcome to be able to change into a looser pair of shorts after each stage. The T-shirt was a mixed blessing as temperature variations throughout each night made it difficult to decide whether or not to keep it: it was too warm in the first few hours of sleep or rest when in the sleeping bag, yet seemingly not warm enough in the cold early hours. The Adidas sandal was necessary (some had brought the hotel's slippers but these didn't last) but I kept wishing I hadn't cut off the back which would have held it better to my foot when going backwards and forwards to the medical and communications tents. Having said that, foot bandaging would have made it difficult to put on the uncut sandal in the first place.

Cooking equipment

A 750ml Esbit titanium cooking pot, a small Esbit titanium foldable stand and a cheap lighter would allow me to boil up enough water to rehydrate my freeze-dried meal each evening. I would collect my pre-ordered solid fuel tablets from the race organisers in Morocco. An Esbit foldable titanium spork would complete all the kit I needed to cook up a meal.

Post-race comment: a windbreak was often necessary and I kept having to borrow my tent mates' large piece of aluminium baking foil to do the job. I would bring that next time. Digging a small hole was another option to put the stove into but successfully doing so depended on whether we were staying overight in a rocky or a sandy area.

Hygiene

Other than compulsory medical kit items (see Appendix 1) I took very little on the hygiene side of things:

- a pack of Orbit Complete Spearmint gum to replace the need for a toothbrush and toothpaste (and hence reduce hand-to-mouth infection over a week);
- a small bottle of alcohol hand gel for use only before every meal and after every toilet visit;
- a few one pound coin-sized Wemmi Wet Wipes which when a drop of water is added expand to become small wet towels for a quick wipe over.

Post-race comment: watching the Wemmi Wet Wipe expand was a pleasure in itself, as was using it to wipe over a hot sandy face. Compared to others across the camp I seemed to have suffered relatively little in the way of diarrhoea and vomiting problems.

Sleeping equipment

The Mammut Ajungilak Sphere Spring was my sleeping bag of choice: with the desert environment being so dry this featherlight down sleeping bag was the way to go with little weight to carry (530 grammes) and a comfort limit down to 0C.

Underneath this I would put a Thermarest NeoAir XLite to give some comfort from a cold, stony desert floor.

Post-race comment: I found it too easy to roll off the Thermarest onto a rocky ground and any kind of movement while sleeping on it sounded like I was rolling around on a giant crisp packet. Adjusting the air in it seemed to help a little. The sleeping bag felt very snug, maybe too much: I felt as if I were wrapped up in rolls of cling film with little ability to move. Then it was too hot, then it was too cold. Maybe that's just how it is when trying to sleep in the desert!

Appendix 4

How to Enter and Recommended Suppliers

Entering the Marathon des Sables

Running the Sahara Ltd is the official Marathon des Sables representative for the United Kingdom, Ireland, South Africa, Israel, Saudi Arabia, United Arab Emirates, Qatar, Bahrain and Kuwait.

Taken from their own website: "No one can deny that finishing the MdS is an incredible accomplishment. But more importantly, you will walk away with a new slant on life – that you can achieve anything you set your mind to do... You will experience something unique, something you will never forget. You will make lifelong friends. You will push your mind and body to the limit. You will find things out about yourself. And in all likelihood you'll get kissed (twice!) by a Frenchman."

Go on, you know you want to...

Telephone: 08444 874 064
Email: mail@marathondessables.co.uk
Website: www.marathondessables.co.uk

Prospective entrants from other countries should visit www.darbaroud.com/en/

Rory Coleman

The only Brit to have completed, thus far, 10 editions of the Marathon des Sables, and now aiming at his 11th at the time of

writing, any question on this event can be answered by Rory. Rory offers highly effective performance coaching for all manner of events as well as the MdS.
Telephone: 02920 255822
Email: rory@rorycoleman.co.uk
Website: www.rorycoleman.co.uk

Likeys
Suppliers of clothing and equipment specific for a variety of extreme events. In their own words "Likeys.com was created to cater for those passionate enough about extreme ultra racing in weird and wonderful climates such as the Arctic, Deserts and Jungles of the World."
Likeys Ltd
No. 2
The Struet
Brecon
Powys
LD3 7LH
Telephone: 01874 622900
Email: sales@likeys.com
Website: www.likeys.com

Sandbaggers
Manufacturer and suppliers of the famous knee-length sand gaiters, ever-popular on the Marathon des Sables, Sandbaggers "are the desert running experts!"
Telephone: 0131 660 3000
Email: gear@sandbaggers.co.uk
Website: www.sandbaggers.co.uk

Complete Morocco
This UK-based travel company arranges trips to Morocco and

introduced for the Marathon des Sables 2012 a Friends and Family package for those wanting to see their loved ones cross the finish line, a very welcome sight for a competitor!

Contact: Janine Hewett
Complete Morocco
46 Malvern Close
Melksham
Wiltshire
SN12 7RR
Telephone: 01225 706665
Email: janine@completemorocco.com
Website: www.completemorocco.com

Jim Mason

Based in Leeds Jim is the most effective sports massage therapist I've known. Jim has treated members of the England Rugby League squad (during the 2011/2012 season) and Leeds Rhinos and a multitude of other athletes from a variety of disciplines, and non-athletes!

Telephone: 0113 887 4655
Email: info@sportsmassgeleeds.co.uk
Website: www.sportsmassageleeds.co.uk

Dr. Martyn Speight

An accomplished amateur fell runner, Dr. Speight specialises in musculoskeletal conditions and sports injuries and sees patients from both a sports and non-sports background.

The Wharfedale Clinic
Barden House
50 Park Road
Guiseley
Leeds
LS20 8AR

Telephone: 01943 850950/878338
Email: info@wharfedaleclinic.co.uk
Website: www.wharfedaleclinic.co.uk

Mr. Andrew Horwood
One of a few musculoskeletal podiatrists I've seen over the years but the only one to have solved my running podiatry problems in conjunction with Dr. Martyn Speight.
See the contact details above for Dr. Martyn Speight.

Appendix 5

Bibliography and Useful Resources

The following resources were used in learning about and training for the Marathon des Sables 2012 and, in part, in writing this book.

Websites

www.marathondessables.co.uk
The website of the UK representative for the Marathon des Sables.

www.themds.co.uk
A forum for Marathon des Sables entrants and veterans with sections on other extreme races.

www.darbaroud.com
The French website of the organisers of the Marathon des Sables.

www.likeys.com
An online shop for all kit and equipment useful for desert ultras and others including a handy Desert Kit List.

www.ldwa.org.uk
Here can be found a page listing off-road Challenge events of various distances open to runners as well as walkers.

http://www.snagfilms.com/films/title/marathon_of_the_sands
A 47 minute film on the 1999 14th Marathon des Sables.

http://www.irunfar.com/2012/04/patrick-bauer-marathon-des-sables-race-director-interview.html
A 2012 interview on the irunfar website with race director Patrick Bauer, by MdS winner Meghan Hicks.

http://ultramadness.co.uk
A website of entertaining blogs on ultra-running set up and written by, amongst others, fellow MdS 2012 competitor and tent mate Wayne Singleton. I came across this blog website in the final stages of writing this book and was delighted to see another one of us had had similar reflections on returning home from the MdS: see the blog entry "After the MdS – recovery and post-race reflection/Monday 16th April – Homeward Bound" dated April 13, 2013.

Books

Survival of the Fittest: Understanding Health and Peak Physical Performance by Mike Stroud (Yellow Jersey Press, 2004; Kindle)
ISBN-10 0224075071

Born to Run: The Hidden Tribe, the Ultra-Runners, and the Greatest Race the World Has Never Seen by Christopher McDougall (Profile Books, 2010)
ISBN-10 1861978774

Why We Run by Robin Harvie (John Murray, 2012; Kindle)
ISBN-10 1848541775

24th Marathon des Sables: A Competitor's Tale by Steve Cushing (Matador, 2010)
ISBN-10 1848762860